TALK
LANGUAGE

How to Use Conversation for Profit and Pleasure

Allan Pease
Alan Garner

PEASE INTERNATIONAL

Published by Pease International

Pease International, P.O. Box 1260, Buderim, QLD 4556, Australia
Tel: + 61 7 5445 5600 Fax: + 61 7 5445 5688
Email: info@peaseinternational.com
www.peaseinternational.com

Pease International UK

Liberty House, 16 Newbold Terrace, Leamington Spa, CV32 4EG, UK
Tel: + 44 1926 889900 Fax: + 44 1926 421100
Email: ukoffice@peaseinternational.com

National Library of Australia
Catalogue-in-Publication data
Pease, Allan, Garner, Alan
Talk Language
ISBN 1 920816 03 8

1. Verbal Communication (Psychology)
Psychology of L. Title 158'.2
Edited by Jacqueline Kent
Concept by Allan Pease
Illustrations by John Hepworth
Cartoons by Paul Zanetti
Cover Design by Tiffany Cruickshank, Trovato Design
Printed by McPherson's Printing Group

Distributed in Australia and New Zealand by HarperCollins Publishers Pty Ltd
Distributed in Asia by Pansing Distribution
Distributed in Hong Kong by Publishers Association Ltd
Distributed in South Africa by Oxford University Press

www.peaseinternational.com

Contents

Why not use Allan Pease as guest speaker for your next conference or seminar?

Pease International Pty Ltd (Australia)
Pease International Ltd (UK)

PO Box 1260
Buderim 4556
Queensland
AUSTRALIA
Tel: ++61 (7) 5445 5600
Fax: ++61 (7) 5445 5688

Liberty House
16 Newbold Terrace
Leamington Spa CV32 4EG
UNITED KINGDOM
Tel: ++44 1926 889900
Fax: ++44 1926 421100

Email: (Aust)   info@peaseinternational.com
         (UK)   ukoffice@peaseinternational.com
Website: www.peaseinternational.com

Also by Allan Pease:

Video Programs
Body Language Series
Silent Signals
How to Make Appointments by Telephone
The Interview

DVD Programs

The Best of Body Language
How to Develop Powerful Communication Skills—Managing the Differences
   Between Men and Women

Audio Programs
The Four Personality Styles
How to Make Appointments by Telephone
How to Remember Names, Faces & Lists
Why Men Don't Listen & Women Can't Read Maps
Questions Are The Answers
The Definitive Book of Body Language
Why Men Lie & Women Cry

Books
The Definitive Book of Body Language
Talk Language
Write Language
Questions are the Answers
Why Men Don't Listen and Women Can't Read Maps
Why Men Don't Have A Clue & Women Always Need More Shoes
Why Men Can Only Do One Thing At A Time & Women Never Stop Talking
The Bumper Book of Rude & Politically Incorrect Jokes
Politically Incorrect Jokes Men Love
How Compatible Are You?– Your Relationship Quiz Book

Acknowledgements

We wish to thank the following people who have directly or indirectly contributed to this book:

Dr Gerald Kranzler, Richard Otton, Dr Susan Glaser, David and Jan Goodwin, Arlene Antonoff, Chris Corck, David Rose, Matthew Braund, Elliot Frohman, Peter Opie, Gay Huber, Sam and Susan Cooper, Steve Tokoly, Rob Winch, Ian McKillop, Dr Waldo Phelps, Gary Goldstein, Jack Curtis, Jack and Myra Moskowitz, Rob Edmonds, John Cooke, Delia Mills, Sue Brannigan, George Manning, Ray Pease, Craig Chapman, Ray Raines, Gabriele Wulser, Jacqueline Kent, Vicki Pease.

Introduction

Each week, you probably have more opportunity for personal contact with strangers, neighbours, friends, family members, children and fellow workers than your medieval ancestors had in their lifetime. Yet your training for all this interaction is almost the same as theirs — practically nothing.

When you were growing up, adults taught you how to read, write, add and subtract. As they corrected you, you mastered those skills. Conversational skills were another matter. You were taught to pronounce words and to organise those words into sentences, but nobody ever taught you how to communicate effectively with other people. When you made mistakes, you weren't shown how to improve — or even told that you needed improvement. Consequently, many people you met didn't warm to you as much as they might have done, or they went away and sought other company. In business, your associates or customers preferred to do their business with someone with whom they felt comfortable.

This experience is not uncommon. In fact, it's normal. According to researchers in communication and psychology, most people throughout their lives continue to make many of the same simple errors they made as children. Very few of us are as good as we might be at making contact with others, turning acquaintances into friends or putting warmth and vitality into long-term relationships.

Research has identified some specific skills vital for the personal effectiveness that few people have fully developed.

Further, it has been found that these skills can be learned in a relatively short time. Unfortunately, these findings have appeared mainly in academic journals and the associated skills are taught by a limited number of teachers.

This book combines two courses designed to fill this gap and to teach conversational skills to everyone in an interesting, straightforward and simple way. Alan Garner developed his course 'Conversationally Speaking: Training for Greater Social Effectiveness' in North America, and it has grown into a network of certified instructors teaching tens of thousands of people in the USA.

In Australia, Allan Pease developed his course 'Techniques and Strategies for Face-to-Face Encounters' to teach people how to use verbal and non-verbal skills in business to persuade, sell, negotiate and interview.

After much contemplation and discussion, these courses have been combined and translated into book form. A course is usually conducted over a period of days or weeks, giving the participants ample opportunity to practise the skills and to integrate them into their lives, whereas a book can be put down or forgotten. Just as reading a book about skiing won't alone make you a more skilful skier and reading a book about body-building won't by itself improve your muscle tone, simply reading this book won't do much for your conversational skills. It will take dedicated reading and a lot of consistent, dedicated practice. We suggest you read no more than one chapter at a time and begin using each skill as soon as you learn it.

We have enjoyed writing this book and we know you'll be excited by the visible improvements you'll find in your everyday life as you become more and more socially effective.

ALLAN PEASE
ALAN GARNER

One

Metalanguage or How to Read Between the Lines

In his book *Body Language—How to Read Others' Thoughts by Their Gestures*, Allan Pease presented a practical guide to the relatively unexplored area of body signals and their relationship to people's attitudes. He stated that researchers generally agree that 60 to 80 per cent of face-to-face communication is conveyed via the non-verbal channel, the balance being done through verbal and vocal channels. In this chapter we will examine the almost totally neglected area of metalanguage — words and phrases that can reveal a person's true attitudes. Like body language, metalanguage gives rise to 'gut feelings', 'intuitions', 'the sixth sense' and 'hunches' that the speaker does not mean what he said. Although this is still a somewhat grey area of interpersonal communication, this chapter attempts to simplify many of the basic words, phrases and expressions that most of us use to communicate a message and, at the same time, it avoids being over-simplistic in such a complex area. Most of the words and phrases covered here are recognised and used by most people but few metawords, if any, are ever consciously interpreted to discover the real feelings behind them.

The *Macquarie Dictionary* defines 'metalanguage' as 'a language which encodes ideas other than the one of the naturally occurring language'. In other words, it is a language hidden within the language. We have all stood at a department store counter waiting for service only to be greeted with, 'Are you right?' from the salesperson. In meta this translates into, 'Is it really necessary for you to disturb me at this time?', and this is the feeling that we subconsciously receive.

Real estate advertisements often contain metalanguage to make a property sound more desirable. Here are some examples, with their real meanings.

Metalanguage	Translation
Unique opportunity to purchase	We are having difficulty selling
An interesting	An ugly
Compact	Very small
Cottage-style	Poky

Residence with great potential	Fallen-down dump
Situate	Situated
In an exclusive, quiet area	A long way from shops and schools
This unique, sought-after property	This ordinary-looking property
Comprises spacious hall, cosy lounge room, 3 bedrooms and modern kitchen	Comprises small hall, tiny lounge room, 3 bedrooms with no wardrobes and kitchen with new paint
Transport at door	Transport stops two metres from front door
Bright sunny outlook	Faces west
On to low-maintenance yard	Has no yard
Many original features	Has outside toilet and laundry
Ideal for the handyman	Will cost a fortune to renovate

Some Irritaters

Some of the most irritating metawords and phrases are 'you know', 'sort of' and 'kind of'. These insidious phrases are more prevalent among the less affluent and less well-educated members of society; they can be heard on many talkback radio shows.

Here is a typical example of a radio program that solicits listeners to phone in and discuss personal or topical subjects. The program runs on Sunday evenings and is conducted by a well-known priest. More often than not, a young teenage girl who finds herself pregnant and cannot locate the child's father calls in for advice. Rather than saying, 'I'm pregnant, what should I do?' the conversation usually follows this pattern.

CALLER: I went out with a boy and now I'm . . . you know!

PRIEST: No, I don't know.

CALLER: Well, he took me back to his place and then he kissed me and then he sort of . . . well . . . you know!

PRIEST: No, I don't know. Exactly what happened?

CALLER: Well after he kissed me, see, he kinda . . . you know . . . and now I'm . . . kinda . . . sorta . . . you know . . . and I don't know what to do.

The caller finished her sentence by raising her voice on the word 'do' leaving the listeners wondering whether she was asking a question or making a statement or whether she had even finished speaking. Admittedly, this stunted form of conversation is extreme rather than usual and highlights the phrase 'you know', which shows lack of confidence in what the speaker is saying and which prods the listener to signal his understanding with the 'yeah, yeah' cliché.

'You know' is so annoying because it is a way of saying, 'I know I am not expressing myself clearly but you are intelligent enough to know what I mean'. 'Sort of' and 'Kinda' are an apology for now knowing the correct word to use.

Why Metalanguage?

If we took all the metalanguage from day-to-day conversation we would be left with short, sharp, to-the-point conversations and we would all sound rude, crude and ignorant towards each other. Metalanguage softens the blows we give each other, lets us secretly manipulate, expose our own virtues or vent an array of emotions without being blatantly rude. Two strangers begin with small talk which is a ritual of conversational phrases, questions, clichés and statements that allow time for them to evaluate whether they can develop a relationship. It usually begins with 'How are you?' which elicits the cliché, 'Fine' to which the enquirer responds, 'That's good' or similar. So rehearsed is this opening ritual that an answer of, 'My mother just died,' would often bring the same answer, 'That's good.' Parting rituals are similar with, 'See ya' being the most common. 'Pleased to have met you,' is used when we do not intend to continue the relationship in the future.

Metalanguage makes prejudices easy to spot. How many times have you seen public toilets marked 'Men' and 'Ladies?' This reveals a prejudice against men by implying that they are not gentlemen or towards women by implying that, where men are men, women are ladies. Metalanguage is everywhere; as well as playing an important part in developing relationships, like body language it is a tool that can be used to uncover a person's real attitude.

For example, most men know that when a lady says, 'No', she means, 'Maybe', and when she says, 'Maybe', she means, 'Yes', but if she says, 'Yes', she's no lady. This old joke demonstrates that what is *said* is not necessarily what is *meant*.

With each new generation, new metawords appear and old ones fade from use. During the 1920s to 1940s the most popular metawords and phrases were 'definitely' and 'sort of thing.' 'Definitely' was used to emphasise the right word, eg, 'You are definitely correct'. This overemphasis can cause suspicion about the speaker's intention; he probably needs to exaggerate his words because of his uncertainty about their credibility. 'Sort of thing' was an apology for possibly using the wrong word; in modern English it has been replaced by 'if you like', while definitely has been replaced by 'actually'. 'Actually, I disagree' can be answered with 'Actually, I don't care.'

As the twentieth century comes to a close, more and more metalanguage is being used in business. One hundred years ago an employer could fire an employee by shouting, 'Get out, you lazy slob!' or the equivalent, but pressures exerted by unions and other bodies have prevented this type of approach and have brought metalanguage into prominence. Today, the lazy employee would receive a company circular that reads something like this: 'Due to extensive reorganisation of this company's export division it has been necessary to amalgamate the positions of stamp-licker and coffee-maker for the benefit of all employees and for the good of the company in general. Chief stamp-licker Joe Bloggs has decided to relinquish his title and seek employment on the open market, where his skills and experience should hold him in good stead.' It still means, 'Get out, you lazy slob!' but the metalanguage is more palatable to the other employees and keeps the unions at bay.

Words are Not the Key

Words alone carry few if any emotional messages. Like words on a computer screen, they convey only facts and information. Words account for a maximum impact of only 7 per cent in a face-to-face conversation. When they are written down they become emotionless; it is easy to see why a courtroom transcript can send an innocent person to jail. The real truth is in the understanding of context, circumstances and use of the words.

Consequently, more public debate arises over an issue

reported in newspaper print than in any other media form, as the reader interprets the words used individually and personally. What one person reads is not necessarily interpreted in the same way by another person. Allan Pease found this when his seven-year-old son Cameron was staying with his grandmother during school holidays. Like most seven-year-old boys, he had learned several 'tough' words at school and was using them in the presence of his grandmother. She decided to put her foot down.

GRANDMOTHER: Cameron, there are two words that *I don't* want to hear in *this* house. One is 'crap' and the other is 'red hot.'

CAMERON: OK, Grandma. What are the two words?

He thought she was describing the two particular words and, because she put her emphasis on the words 'don't' and 'this', he decoded that it was all right to continue using the two words in question as long as his grandmother didn't hear them in that particular house. He continued to use them in every other location, and only around her when she was in someone else's house. This is a classic example of how misuse and misinterpretation of words can lead to strained relationships.

Words and Emotional Attachment

The word 'my' a signals the speaker's emotional involvement with the words that follow. For example, 'my wife' shows an emotional attachment, whereas 'the wife', which turns her into an object, denies emotional attachment and even shows contempt or hostility. 'My boss' indicates an emotional link with the boss, whereas 'the boss' puts him at a distance. 'My country is financially depressed', shows a deep-seated concern for the problem, as opposed to, 'Australia is financially depressed' which says, 'It's their problem, not mine'.

The words 'with' and 'to' also indicate distance between

people. If someone talks 'to' you, it puts you at a distance and probably means that that person is going to talk 'at' you. The word 'to' carries such strong emotional overtones that we use the phrase 'a good talking to' meaning a reprimand. Talking 'with', on the other hand, indicates that we are communicating together and our conversation will be productive. To tell a person that you wish to talk 'to' him or her is likely to put barriers between you. Talking 'with' people is more likely to get co-operation.

In a recent negotiation, one man threatened to terminate the discussion and said, 'We will have to go our separate ways.' This phrase is used between parting lovers, not professional business people and it alerted the other party to the fact that the man felt he had a personal or emotional attachment to him. The other man changed his negotiating position from an impersonal financial approach to a person-to-person basis. This worked, and the negotiation was completed to their mutual satisfaction.

Emphasis on a Word

Changing the emphasis on each word in a sentence can completely alter the meaning of the sentence. Read the sentences below, putting the emphasis on the words in italics, and notice the changes in meaning.

'*I* should accept that job.' (*I should accept it rather than you.*)

'I *should* accept that job.' (*I should accept it rather than something else.*)

'I should *accept* that job.' (*I should accept it rather than criticise or reject it.*)

'I should accept *that* job.' (*and no other*)

'I should accept that *job*.' (*I have contempt for it.*)

This example shows that it is possible to manipulate what people hear by emphasising different words, and how newspaper stories can be misconstrued.

Read the following question to another person with emphasis on the italicised words and listen to the answer: 'How many animals of *each species* did Moses take on to the Ark?' Most people give a numerical answer to the question and those who think it through usually answer, 'Two'. The answer is, in fact, none. Moses never had an Ark; it belonged to Noah. When you put the emphasis on 'each species' you get a different answer than if you emphasised 'Moses', where the trick may become obvious.

Here's another example: 'When in history did Australia begin with an "A" and end with an "E"?' The answer is, 'Always'. The word 'Australia' always started with an A, and the word 'end' always began with an 'E'. When the emphasis is put on 'Australia', the listener is fooled into giving the wrong answer.

Just as the listener is manipulated into giving a predetermined answer to the question, much of our day-to-day conversation with others has the predetermined objective of manipulating the listener. This is often an unconscious manipulation, and we will now examine some of the ways in which it is done.

Clichés

Just as people develop repetitive, annoying body language habits, they also use stale and wornout phrases called clichés, which can either end a conversation or encourage the listener to volunteer a cliché of his own. Clichés are prepackaged words and sayings used by unimaginative people or by those who are too lazy to describe a situation perceptively. (Platitudes and truisms are other kinds of clichés.)

Clichés can give useful clues to the speaker's thoughts. For example, 'incidentally' is an apology for an irrelevance and is one of the most used clichés in modern English. 'Incidentally' comes in several other forms, including, 'by the way', 'before I forget', 'while I think of it', and 'I was just wondering'. It is intended to play down the importance of what the speaker is about to say, for example, 'Thanks for the loan of your car — incidentally, was that dent always in your bumper bar?' In this case, 'incidentally' is used to hide the fact that the question about the damaged bumper bar is the most important thing being said.

'Incidentally' alerts you that the words following it are the key point in the statement.

'John, we really appreciated the work you've done on the project and you did a good job. Incidentally, your week's vacation has been postponed till next month.'

What can you do about clichés if you are guilty of using them? The best idea is to drop them from your vocabulary. If that is difficult, alter them to a humorous version that can be quite refreshing to your listeners. For example, 'A bird in the hand is worth two in the bush' can be changed to, 'A bush in the hand is worth two birds'. 'Behind every man there's a woman' can be perked up by adding, 'often it's the other woman'. But the best advice for keeping a conversation open is to drop clichés, truisms and platitudes altogether and practise thinking imaginatively. At first, this is not easy to do, but it will improve the quality of your conversation.

Single-word Metalanguage

Let us examine some of the most commonly used metawords that signal that a person may be attempting to disguise the truth or to mislead. 'Honestly,' 'sincerely' and 'frankly' indicate that the speaker is about to be considerably less frank, less honest or less sincere than he claims. Perceptive people unconsciously decode these words and get a 'gut feeling' that the speaker is trying to deceive them. For example, 'Frankly, this is the best offer I can give you', translates to, 'It's not the best offer but maybe you'll believe it.' 'I love you' is more believable than 'I honestly love you'. 'Undoubtedly' gives reason to doubt; 'without a doubt' is definite.

Many people develop the habit of using these types of word. They often use them to preface an honest statement, which can have the detrimental effect of making the statement sound untrue. Ask your friends, relations and co-workers if they have noticed any of these metawords in your speech, and if they have (which is likely), you will begin to understand why some people never seem to be able to develop a trusting relationship with you. The words, 'OK' and 'right' force the listener to agree with the speaker's point of view: 'You'd agree with that, right?'. The listener is forced to respond with his own 'right' even if he doesn't necessarily agree with the speaker's point of view. 'Right' also shows doubt about the listener's ability to receive and clearly understand what is being discussed.

The words 'just' and 'only' are used to minimise the significance of the words that follow. 'I'll only take five minutes of your time' is used by time-wasters and others who wish to take up to an hour of your time, whereas, 'I'll take five minutes of your time' is specific and more believable. The word 'only' is only used to relieve a person's guilt or to put the blame for unpleasant consequences elsewhere. For example, a mother recently locked her baby in the car while she shopped at the supermarket. The temperature was 35°C and unfortunately the baby died of heat exhaustion. When the mother was interviewed by the press she said, 'I was only gone ten minutes'. The word 'only' relieved her of much of the blame. Had she said, 'I was gone ten minutes' she would have sounded guilty and been severely criticised for her irresponsibility. (In metalanguage, 'ten minutes' usually means an unspecified amount of time between twenty and sixty minutes.)

'Only $9.95' and 'just $40 deposit' are used to convince the listener or reader that the price charged is insignificant. 'I'm only human' is the catchphrase of someone who doesn't want to take responsibility for his or her blunders; 'I just wanted to tell you I love you' masks the timid lover's need to say, 'I love you'.

Whenever you hear someone use 'only' or 'just', you need

to consider why that person is attempting to minimise the importance of what he or she is saying. Is it because people lack the confidence to say what they really feel? Are they intentionally trying to deceive? Are they trying to avoid their responsibilities? Close examination of 'only' and 'just', related to the context in which they occur, can reveal the answer.

'Try' is frequently used by people who are habitual under-achievers and failures to announce in advance that they may not succeed at a task, or that they even expect to fail. When a person is asked to complete a difficult task he may say, 'I'll try' or its equivalent, 'I'll do my best', both of which signal impending failure. Translated, these expressions mean, 'I have doubts about my ability to do it.' When the person ultimately fails or ruins the project he says, 'Well, I tried', confirming that he had little confidence in his ability to handle the job. 'I was only trying to help' is the phrase used by nosy meddlers and gossips who are caught up in someone else's business. In context, 'only' attempts to minimise intentional involvement, and 'try' indicates that he did not necessarily intend to help relieve the problem. An eager man who makes an improper pass at a woman and gets his face slapped may use, 'I was only trying to be friendly' to cover up his poor techniques.

'We'll look into it', 'We will make every effort' and, 'I'll see what I can do' are the favourites of corporate executives and government officials who want to pass the buck.

When you hear these phrases in conversation, ask the person to commit himself to a 'will' or 'will not' attitude before you assign a task. It is better that a person 'will not' attempt an assignment than that he should 'try' and fail. 'Try' is about as reassuring as a 'definite maybe'.

Two-word Metalanguage

'Yes, but', is an attempt to avoid intimidation by feigning agreement. 'But' generally contradicts the words that come before it or signals that the person has lied up to that point. 'Your wife is a lady, but . . .' (but she's not). 'Yes, but' can also be expressed as, 'however', or 'still'. 'I accept what you've said; however . . .' (I don't accept what you've said). 'That dress looks very nice, still . . .' (I hate it).

'With respect', which also appears as 'with all due respect' means, quite clearly, that the speaker has little or no respect for the listener and even contempt for him or her. 'I appreciate your comments, sir, but may I say, with respect, that I disagree.' This is a long-winded way of saying, 'What a load of bull' and is intended to deliver a blow to the listener, whilst cushioning his fall.

Have you ever had a conversation in which the speaker sounded convincing but the more he spoke, the less convincing you found him? There's a good chance that the speaker was using 'believe me', another contradictory example of two-word meta. 'Believe me, this is the best offer you'll get' often means, 'If I can get you to believe me, you'll buy now and not shop around'. If a person is likely to lie, he reveals his deceit through metalanguage. The degree to which 'believe me' tries to convince is proportionate to the extent of the deceit. The speaker feels that you won't believe him or that what he is saying is unbelievable, so he prefaces his remarks with, 'Believe me'. 'I'm not kidding' and 'Would I lie to you?' are other versions of 'Believe me'. The ultimate lie sounds like this: 'Believe me, I'm not kidding. Would I lie to you?' (*Just give me half a chance!*)

One of the most widely used phrases in any conversation is 'of course', which has three common meanings. 'You must be a fool to have asked that question' (sarcastic); 'I am so well-informed that I know all there is to know about this' (showing off); 'I know you are intelligent enough to know this, but I'll mention it anyway' (polite). It is most often used to introduce an assumption the speaker wants the listener to make. 'Of course, I'd expect my usual 10 per cent discount' is an example of the speaker giving his opinion prefaced by 'of course' which assumes that the listener also shares the same opinion. 'Of course' infers that the statements that follow are normal practice. It is often a device used to get one's own way by implying that everyone else agrees. When a negotiator says, 'Of course, we will not hold you to those terms', it often means, 'Yes, we will'.

Let us now analyse some of the common expressions and phrases to examine their likely metalanguage translations.

Manipulators and set-ups

Manipulative metalanguage reveals a person's intent to push you into something that he wants or to get his own way. 'Don't you think that', 'Don't you feel' and 'Isn't it true that' ask for a 'yes' from the listener and allow the speaker to manipulate. 'As you may be aware' and 'no doubt' are intended to achieve a similar end and to give the listener credit for being smart enough to *be* aware, or to imply that the listener already knows the facts. 'Out of the goodness of my heart' is a real con, alerting you to the speaker's potentially unsavoury intentions. It is also used to relieve the guilty conscience of someone who gives money at the door after being embarrassed by a persistent collector. 'Should' translates to 'in my opinion' and is one of the most manipulative words in the English language. 'No doubt you are aware that you should do the right thing' means, 'Do exactly what I want'.

Then there are the gossips and blabbermouths whose main reason for existence seems to be to spread and embellish all rumours they can hear or invent. So overwhelming is their desire to give information that they subconsciously attempt to hide it with, 'You won't believe this, but' 'I shouldn't be telling you this, but' and, 'Don't breathe a word of this'. 'I don't want to start rumours' usually means, 'I love starting rumours'; 'I don't want to hear any idle gossip', often means, 'Get straight to the juicy bits'; 'I know it's none of my business' means, 'Let me see if I can pry into this'.

'I would hope' is a clever way of not giving an opinion, whilst sounding as though you are giving an opinion. A well-known politician said recently, 'I would hope that taxation will not increase for the rest of the year.' The word 'would' means 'under normal circumstances' and 'hope' means wishful thoughts, that is, he doesn't expect it to happen. Translated, his words meant, 'Under normal circumstances I would not want taxation levels to increase, but they probably will, anyway.' Two months after this statement was made, taxation on pensions and personal assets were introduced.

'I could say something about that' lures the listener into replying, 'Well, go on, then!' It has two uses; humorous, or as a set-up for an argument. In a humorous context it seeks the reply, 'Say it' and having said it, the listeners have a duty to laugh. In provoking a fight or argument it sounds like this:

BOB: Sue is such a good-natured, clean-living girl. (*Pays a third-party compliment*)

SALLY: I could say something about that. (*Set-up*)

BOB: (Quizzically) What do you mean? (*Bites, hook, line and sinker*)

SALLY: I don't want to start rumours, but . . . (*Here's a juicy bit of gossip about Sue*)

Bob would have done better to ignore the set-up, change the subject or terminate the conversation. Sally threw him a line on which he has bitten, and he is about to be reeled in and gutted like a fish.

Two other favourites are, 'Don't get me wrong' meaning, 'You won't like what I'm about to say but I don't care' and 'It's not the money, it's the principle' which usually means, 'It's the money.' (This one tells you to check your wallet before the speaker departs.)

Ego Trippers

Conditioning from childhood prevents most people from saying things like 'I'm talented', 'I'm capable', 'I'm good' or making other such ego-building statements. Even though most people are prevented from uttering such words by invisible third parties such as 'them', 'everyone' and, 'the public generally', the desire to say, 'I'm good' becomes apparent in metalanguage. An over-inflated ego is painfully obvious with 'In my humble opinion,' which is the favourite of older egotists, whereas the younger bigheads use 'If you ask my opinion' to show their self-importance, when nobody has asked for their opinion. Other versions include 'Far be it for me to disagree,' or, 'Maybe it's not my place to say this, but . . .' which are used to preface some great deep meaningful thought that the listener had better like.

In the business world, many executives attempt to conceal their sense of self-importance with 'off the top of my head' which allows a hopeless suggestion to pass over quietly and a good one to be artificially highlighted, allowing the executive to appear to be a genius who can be brilliant 'at the drop of a hat'.

The super-inflated ego is identified by the person who refers to himself in the royal third person singular. Recently, at a convention, a senior executive we shall call Bob Brown said, 'Bob Brown is here to serve the company and his door is always open.' The real message here is, 'I am here to be revered, adored, cherished and worshipped.'

Those with over-inflated egos have their own ways of sounding important, even when they are not involved in a particular project. An egomaniac was asked to contribute to a fund for starving people in the Third World and told the collector that he had 'done what I could in my own way', which sounds mysteriously impressive. When pressed to reveal what he had done, he said he had stopped over for a weekend in India on his way to a skiiing holiday in Switzerland and was so appalled by the poverty he saw that he recommended sponsorship of Third World children to other people. The real message in this metalanguage was, 'I'm better, smarter, richer and more dynamic than you.' (He ended his statement by saying 'We've talked for long enough about me. Let's hear from you. What do you think of my new Mercedes?')

Interesters and Persuaders

Interesters are used to keeping a dull conversation rolling and are favourites of those who feel insecure about what they are saying, probably because it is uninteresting, or because they suffer from verbal diarrhoea. 'Did you hear the one about' is a cliché used by those who are poor joke-tellers. It demands a cliché reply of 'no' and instructs the listener to deny any knowledge of the joke and to prepare to laugh at the punchline. Jokes told without this wornout preface receive far more accolades than those prefaced with it; it is never used by professional comedians or raconteurs such as Dave Allen or Johnny Carson. 'Which reminds me of the story about' is used by many public speakers and it suffers the same fate.

'And do you know what he said?' is a boring, repetitive verbal tic used to get the listener involved when the conversation sags. It demands a reply of, 'No, what?' from the listener. 'And guess what happened?' is a similar device. Next time you hear these phrases uttered repetitively, answer, 'No, and I don't care', and watch the reaction. You will be surprised how many people will ignore your comment and keep talking.

Persuaders attempt to force agreement with the speaker's point of view and reveal insights into the speaker's attitudes, thoughts and prejudices. 'What do you think of' is followed by the speaker's personal feelings about a subject. When a retired person asks, 'What do you think of the new tax on pensions for retirees?' it translates to, 'I'm against it' and could be handled with the reply, 'That's a good question. What are your thoughts?' which allows you to avoid an argument.

Two phrases that frustrate even the most positive thinkers are, 'Why don't we' and 'Why can't we', followed by a positive statement. 'Why don't we go to the beach?' unwittingly makes the listener's mind begin searching for reasons against going to the beach, whereas, 'Let's go to the beach' is likely to get action. 'Why can't we have the day off, boss?' prompts the boss to think of reasons why you can't have it off. 'Why not!' is an equally negative reply to a positive statement. When a speaker asks, 'Would you like to go out tonight?', the reply, 'Why not!' is intended to mean, 'Yes', but could be decoded as 'No' by the listener.

'Why don't we go to lunch some time?' forces a positive reply and insures that the lunch will never take place. 'Some time' in this context means, 'hopefully never'. It's a great line to use on people whom you don't like very much.

'I think that we all agree' attempts to force you to comply and not argue, whereas 'Let me make one thing perfectly clear' shows contempt for the listener and casts doubt on the listener's intelligence or ability to understand things clearly.

When you know what to listen for, understanding these phrases can be not only useful but a lot of fun.

Popular Metalanguage

Here are some of the popular metaphrases and meta-statements you hear every day. 'I didn't go too far, did I?' means, 'I know I did, but I don't care,' whereas, 'I didn't talk too much, did I?' means, 'I know I did, but please say I didn't' as it demands a 'no' answer from the listener. 'Did I say something wrong?' admits, 'I said something wrong.' 'I was just going to say,' usually means, 'I was not going to say that at all' as in the case of the husband who interrupts his wife's enquiry about his late-night activities with, 'I was just going to say how lovely you look.'

The woman who says, 'I can't go out looking like this' is really saying, 'Don't make me clean up'. Later in his apartment when she whispers, 'I really can't stay' it means, 'I'll stay.' (He has probably invited her into his apartment for 'a coffee' or 'a nightcap', which need little translation to anyone over eighteen years of age.)

'I don't want to seem' is followed by a word describing how the speaker feels. 'I don't want to seem rude,' means, 'I am about to be rude.'

At funerals we all use metalanguage to hide our real feelings. 'What can you say at a time like this?' means, 'I would prefer not to talk about it.' 'If ever I can do anything, just let me know', means, 'Don't call me, I'll call you' and 'He died so young' means, 'I feel insecure about my age.' 'If only' is used to place the blame elsewhere: 'If only the ambulance had been quicker.'

In an argument or debate, statements like, 'Stay out of this!', 'Forget it', 'Subject closed', 'I've heard enough' and 'What's the use' all mean, 'I can't cope with this situation any longer.'

Business Metalanguage

When businessmen and negotiators get together, metalanguage abounds. 'I'm not suggesting you should do this, but' means, 'Do it'. 'Business is business' is an attempt to justify why a person has ripped off another person or to rationalise his own lack of business ethics, whereas, 'In a businesslike manner' says, 'I'll screw you for everything I can get.' 'Let's not beat around the bush' is often the opening phrase that leads to 'business is business' when that person makes an unreasonable demand.

The use of 'if — then' statements can allow a buyer to fob off a salesman by making an unreasonable request. 'If you can deliver by the first of the month, I'll take it' means that the problem is now offloaded onto the salesman and away from the buyer. 'I'll tell you what', and 'Why don't we do this' are often used to preface 'no' to a proposition, 'I'll tell you what, John, I'll think it over and try to get back to you Monday!' The metalanguage here says 'No thanks — don't call me, I'll call you.'

Egos also flourish in many business negotiations. As already noted, 'Off the top of my head' allows a person to seem to have the innate ability to turn out great ideas like popcorn, and, 'It may interest you to know' tells you that I am smarter, wiser or better informed than you. 'Let me put it this way' translates to, 'Here's a distorted version of the facts.'

Here is a typical boss/employee scene.

EMPLOYEE: Boss, I don't want to sound like I'm complaining (*I'm complaining*) but (*confirms the contradiction*) as you know (*patronising*) I haven't had a pay rise in two years and, with respect, (*I have no respect for you*) you should (*my personal opinion*) consider giving me one.

BOSS: It may interest you to know (*I'm smarter*) that I have considered it (*it's now past tense*) and on the whole (*let's not be specific*) your work has been good (*past tense*) but (*contradiction*) you'll have to (*do as I say*) wait and see (*decision postponed*). I'll tell you what (*No!*) I'll sleep on it (*it's not important enough to keep me awake*) and let you know (*I'm smarter*) how I would like to see your job handled for greater productivity (*you're incapable*).

In this scene the employee would walk away saying to himself, 'I tried' (*I didn't expect to succeed*) and the boss thinks, 'Business is business' (*up yours*).

Family Situations

Children are just as sensitive in decoding metalanguage as they are in reading body language. Parents who attempt to talk with their children in adult language are doomed to frustration as children use metalanguage extensively. This frustration with children usually leads to clichés like, 'And don't answer back!' as the adult's last word. 'When I was your age,' kills most dialogue between adult and child, mainly because children do not believe that an adult was ever a child.

'If you don't stop doing that, I'll . . .' and 'How many times have I told you not to do that?' are probably the two biggest turnoffs for most kids.

Metalanguage between adults, however, is easier to understand than that of children. Here's a typical example.
WIFE: How was the convention in Fiji, darling? (*ritual opening*)
HUSBAND: Great. (*I had a good time.*)
WIFE: How was the food? (*lead-up to the main point*)
HUSBAND: Absolutely fantastic! (*Pity you don't feed me like that.*)
WIFE: Meet anyone interesting? (*Did you play up?*)
HUSBAND: The guys I met from head office were really great. And I met a lot of the boys again over cards. (*defensive answer*)
Some time later she is serving dinner; he is hanging a picture.
WIFE: Dinner's ready. (*Come, now.*)
HUSBAND: Just a minute. (*Don't bother me right now.*)
WIFE: It's on the table! (*Come now, you ignoramus.*)
HUSBAND: I'll be right there (*Leave me alone.*)
WIFE: It's going cold! (*I'm about to attack.*)
HUSBAND: All right, all right! I can't seem to get anything finished around here. (*I'm disorganised and I am going to blame you.*)
WIFE: Did I say something wrong? (*I know I did, but don't care.*)

This whole metaconversation might have been avoided if she had asked what time he wanted dinner and he agreed to be there on time.

Political Metalanguage

If metalanguage did not exist, neither would politicians, as they would have little to say. The purpose of political metalanguage is to create an impenetrable wall of words that no one can understand and at the same time make the politician appear to be at least half-intelligent. Analyse this interview with politican Joe Brown.

REPORTER: Could you comment on reports of financial payoffs to members of your government?

JOE BROWN: Let me make one thing perfectly clear. (*I have contempt for you.*) Joe Brown would never allow anything like that (*Revere me, adore me*) in his government.

REPORTER: Have you ever considered (*this is my personal opinion*) a full investigation?

JOE BROWN: Exactly what are you talking about? (*I know exactly what you mean and don't like your attitude.*)

REPORTER: To have your ministers investigated.

JOE BROWN: As you are probably aware (*I'm smarter*) this has already been suggested, but (*contradiction*) believe me (*I'm lying*) when I say I'll do everything possible (*I'll forget about it within five minutes of this interview*) to uncover any ill-doings by ministers. Needless to say (*I don't want what I am about to say to eventuate*) we all want any offenders caught. Don't get me wrong, (*get me wrong*) however, (*contradiction*) I'm not about to axe people over it (*just give me a chance*). I wouldn't want that (*that's what I want*) but (*contradiction*) it goes without saying (*attempt to force agreement*) that government officials should (*in my personal opinion*) be beyond reproach (*exaggeration to get agreement*). Frankly, that's how I feel about it! (*I have not been frank on other issues.*)

Well, (*showing frustration*) all we can say (*hostile opinion*) is thank heavens (*exaggeration*) for metalanguage or most politicians would be looking for alternative careers. It is no surprise that many choose the legal field to practise their metaskills.

Summary

For conversation to be effective it must be flexible, and metalanguage is important in maintaining friendly relationships with others. Prior to reading this chapter you probably felt that the phrases you use as a speaker have no logical relationship to what we are saying but, as you have discovered (*you get the credit*) that is not the case. As you talk with people, become aware of the standard phrases and clichés you use and eliminate or change the ones that impair effective communication. Listen between the lines of what others say and you can develop the knack of seeing through press releases, media blurbs, and the speeches of public figures who seek to manipulate.

Finally, here are some other common metalanguage phrases to listen for.

QUESTION: *How did the election go?*
META-ANSWERS: 1. We did better than at the last election.
2. We increased our share of women's votes.
3. We had more people vote for us than ever before.
4. We fought clean.
TRANSLATION: *We lost.*

QUESTION: *How do you like my new apartment?*
META-ANSWERS: 1. It has that lived-in look.
2. It makes you feel right at home.
3. What an interesting colour scheme.
4. I hate a home where everything is in its proper place.

5. You feel like you can just take off your shoes and relax.

TRANSLATION: *Its' a dump.*

QUESTION: *As my local government representative, will you pursue this matter for me?*

META-ANSWERS:
1. I have listened with interest and taken particular note of your views.
2. At the next opportunity I will make these points perfectly clear to all concerned.
3. Let me assure you that I will keep the matter in the forefront of my mind.
4. I will send you the environmental impact study for your persual.
5. I will look into it as soon as possible.

TRANSLATION: *No way.*

METASTATEMENT: *I'm sorry if I said the wrong thing. I didn't know he was your neighbour.*

META-ANSWERS:
1. That's OK. Forget it.
2. You weren't to know.
3. Don't be embarrassed about it.
4. I'm sure he didn't hear it.

TRANSLATION: *You have neither manners nor tact.*

QUESTION: *How do you like him?*

META-ANSWERS:
1. Frankly, I hardly know him.
2. He's excellent at his job.
3. He means well.
4. He's a snappy dresser, isn't he?
5. I've got nothing against him.
6. Women really go for him.

TRANSLATION: *He is a bastard.*

METASTATEMENT: We, the trade union movement, regret the unfortunate inconvenience caused to you, the general public, by our strike.

TRANSLATION: *We, the trade union movement, regret the unfortunate inconvenience caused to you, the general public, by our strike, but we feel it will get us what we want.*

METASTATEMENT: You must come over to dinner sometime.
TRANSLATION: *Don't come unless you're invited.*

METASTATEMENT: I hope you like Chinese food.
TRANSLATION: *Chinese food is what you are getting, whether you like it or not.*

METASTATEMENT: Please don't mind me.
TRANSLATION: *Please don't mind me, I'm used to being treated like a doormat.*

METASTATEMENT: We're all in this together.
TRANSLATION: *We'll share the blame it it fails and I'll take the credit if it succeeds.*

METAQUESTION: Did you have trouble finding the place?
TRANSLATION: *Why are you so late?*

METASTATEMENT: The standard of this hotel is just as good as it was ten years ago.
TRANSLATION: *The standard of this hotel has not improved in ten years.*

METASTATEMENT: It's not that I don't believe you . . .
TRANSLATION: *It's not that I don't believe you, I just don't trust you.*

METASTATEMENT: I hope I'm not interrupting . . .
TRANSLATION: *I know I'm interrupting, but I'm going to, whether you like it or not.*

METASTATEMENT: We sold twice as much this year.

TRANSLATION: *We only sold half as much last year.*

METASTATEMENT: You really look so slim now.
TRANSLATION: *You really looked so fat before.*

METASTATEMENT: Of course I'm not offended. I can take a joke.
TRANSLATION: *I'll get you for this!*

METASTATEMENT: Yes, the conference was really good, much ground was covered and there was a full and frank exchange of views.
TRANSLATION: *It was a waste of time.*

METASTATEMENT: Here, let me get you an ashtray.
TRANSLATION: *Let me get you an ashtray before you drop any more ash on my carpet, you ignoramus.*

METASTATEMENT: When I found them in bed together, I just didn't know what to think.
TRANSLATION: *When I found them in bed together, I knew exactly what to think!*

Two

How To Ask Questions That Promote Conversation

Your social and business success is directly related to your ability to ask effective questions and get the right responses. In a social situation it makes the difference between winning or losing a potential friend, meeting a new partner or even

successfully talking over the fence to a neighbour. In business
this skill, or lack of it, can make or break a sale, win a
negotiation or determine your success in a job interview.

Everbody knows the frustration of not having the right
question at the right time. Take the case of one man reporting
on his efforts to talk to his neighbours. 'I tried, I really did.
I asked them a question and didn't get much of an answer.
So I asked another. And then another. After a while, I felt
like I was an FBI agent interrogating suspects rather than a
man trying a make pleasant conservation with the people next
door.'

Here is another example. Peter, a computer salesman, is
endeavouring to sell a new system.

PETER: How long have you had this system?

POTENTIAL CLIENT: About eighteen months.

PETER: Are you happy with it?

POTENTIAL CLIENT: Yes, so far.

PETER: Does it handle your direct mail program?

POTENTIAL CLIENT: Yes it does.

PETER: Has your system performed up to your expectations?

POTENTIAL CLIENT: Yes it's been pretty good.

PETER: Where did you purchase the system?

POTENTIAL CLIENT: I got it from the Apple Company.

PETER: Is their service good?

POTENTIAL CLIENT: The system's had no problems, so I
haven't needed the service.

PETER: So you haven't tried their back-up service?

POTENTIAL CLIENT: No.

PETER: I see. Nice day, isn't it?

POTENTIAL CLIENT: Yes. Why don't you go and enjoy it?

Everyone asks questions, but few people know how to do so
in ways that effectively promote conversation. When your
questions elicit little response, the problem may not be that
your conversational partners are unfriendly or uninterested,
or that the situation isn't right. The fault may be in the type
of questions you ask or in the way you phrase them.

There are two types of questions you can ask: closed-ended
and open-ended.

Closed-Ended Questions

Closed-ended questions are like true — false or multiple-choice questions in that they require only a one-or two-word reply. For example: 'Where are you from?'; 'Do you go jogging?'; 'Shall we meet at 5:30, 6:00 or 6:30?'; 'Do you think all nuclear power plants should be shut down?'

Closed-ended questions are valuable for getting others to disclose specific facts about themselves that you may wish to explore in greater detail. 'I was born in the city but grew up in the country'; 'Yes, I jog five kilometres a day'; and for getting them to state definite positions: 'Six o'clock is fine,'; 'I don't want the nuclear plants we have shut down, but I don't favour building any more either.'

While they have a definite role to play, continuous closed-ended questions lead to dull conversation, followed by awkward silences. People who are asked a series of closed-ended questions soon feel as if they are being interrogated by the police.

Open-Ended Questions

You must follow up a closed-ended question with an open-ended one if you want to keep your conversations going and create greater interest and depth. Open-ended questions are like essay questions; they promote answers of more than a few words. They ask for explanations and elaborations, while showing your conversational partners, much to their delight, that you are so interested in what they have said that you want to know more.

For example, once Peter the computer salesman found out that the potential client was happy with his computer system, he might have followed up with one of these open-ended questions: 'How did you happen to choose an Apple system?';

'In what way has the Apple changed your business?'; 'What are your plans for computers in your business in the future?'

Having asked someone where he's from and having found out he's from the country, you might ask him open-ended questions such as, 'How did you happen to move here from the country?'; 'How's the lifestyle in the country different from what we have here?'; 'What was the best part of growing up in the country?'

Having learned that someone favours keeping existing nuclear power plants operating but doesn't want more built, you might ask these open-ended questions: 'How do you think we might deal with the waste produced by the reactors we now have?'; 'What do you feel is the best way for someone to help stop more plants from being built?'; 'If more plants aren't built, what do you think the nation could do to secure additional power?'

You can observe from these examples that open-and closed-ended questions begin, for the most part, with different words. The following lists will help you in starting off questions.

Closed-Ended	Both	Open-Ended
	What?	
Are?		How?
Do?		Why?
Who?		In what way?
When?		Tell me about. . .
Where?		
Which?		

You may consider that some people would probably answer many of the closed-ended questions you've read in an open-ended way. While this is true, your conversational partners are likely to answer open-ended questions at consistently greater length because they actively encourage speaking freely. When you ask open-ended questions, others can relax, knowing that you want them to become involved and to express themselves fully.

Question-Asking Increases Your Control

You need never be stuck in boring conversations because, when you ask questions, you control to a large extent the topics that are discussed. Let's suppose a friend tells you, 'I just got back from France'. Here are some of the many questions you could choose to have him answer, depending upon your interests:

'*What* was the weather like there?'

'*How* did you manage to communicate with the French?'

'*Tell me* the most memorable thing that happened.'

'*How* did you manage to get hotel rooms over there?'

'*In what way* was the food there different from what we have here?'

If a woman introduces herself as a nurse, you could choose from these questions to ask:

'*Why* did you decide to become a nurse?'

'*What* did you have to do to enter the field?'

'*Tell me* some problems that people often come to you with.'

'*What role* are drugs playing with young people today?'

'*How does* listening to troubles all day affect your outlook on life?'

If you don't want to talk about her job, you could openendedly ask, 'What do you do for fun when you're not nursing?'

In choosing which questions to ask, keep two considerations in mind. First, only ask questions when you genuinely want to hear what the other person has to say. No matter how skilful you are, if you just go through the motions, others will eventually sense that you are insincere, merely trying to trick them into liking you.

Second, strive to maintain dual perspective. Having dual perspective means thinking not just in terms of what *you* want to say and hear, but also in terms of the *other person's* interest. The worst bores of all are oblivious to the wants and needs of others. They are best epitomised by a distinguished-looking gentleman saying to a woman at a cocktail party, 'Enough of all this talking about *me*. Let's talk about *you*. What do you think of me so far?'

Being sincere and maintaining dual perspective are tremendously important in effectively using all the other skills that will be covered in this book.

Common Mistakes In Asking Questions

Asking questions that are too open-ended

Melissa, the wife of a salesman, said that her life was becoming boring. Why? 'Because all day long, all I've got for company is a three-year-old and an infant. So when Bob comes home and I ask him, "How'd it go today?" I really want to know. But what does he say? "Oh, the usual." Then he turns on the TV and that's that.' Melissa has been making several simple errors. First, her inquiry is too broad in scope. Asking questions is like turning on taps; the more open they are, the more response you get – up to a point. Very open-ended questions like Melissa's require so much effort and time to answer that most people give up without even trying.

Other examples of this type of frustrating question include, 'What have you been up to lately?' 'Tell me about yourself', and 'What's new?'

Second, 'How'd it go today?' sounds more like a cliché question intended to open the lines of communication than a genuine request for information. Cliché questions generally elicit cliché answers like, 'Pretty good', or 'Not bad.'

Finally, Melissa asked the same question every day. Not only did this add to the likelihood of it being considered a cliche, but the thought of answering the same unimaginative question over and over again probably bored Bob.

It was suggested to Melissa that she read the daily newspaper regularly. Then, after leaving Bob a little time to relax, she could ask him more specific open-ended questions about interesting topics with which he was familiar.

That night, Melissa told Bob she had heard that the local school was thinking about dropping the foreign language requirement for students, so she asked him what he thought about this issue. She said, 'I'm not sure how I feel about it. How do you feel they should handle it?', an open-ended question.

This led to a discussion about whether learning a foreign language helps students better understand other peoples. They shared their own experiences, which led to fun in trying to converse in rusty high school French. Finally, when they were all talked out, Bob gave Melissa a little kiss and whispered, 'Ah madame, you are *magnifique!*' How's that for a successful experiment?

Beginning with Difficult Questions

A real estate agent once revealed this trick of the trade. 'When a potential client walks in the door, I don't ask him what he has in mind. That's too hard a question to start out with. He'd become nervous and withdrawn. And if I pressed him, he would probably withdraw all the way out the door. Instead, I ask what type of home he's living in right now. That puts him at ease, gets him feeling comfortable around me. After a while, either he or I will shift the conversation around to what he's got in mind.'

This advice also applies to social occasions. It's usually best to start with simple questions about topics in which others are likely to be interested, and with which they may be familiar.

Asking leading questions

Leading questions are the most closed-ended possible, in that they only invite agreement on your personal opinion. For instance:

'It's already eight-thirty. Shouldn't we stay home tonight?'

'You don't think they're right, do you?'

'Two hours of TV is enough for one evening, don't you think?'

Asking leading questions in court has earned many a lawyer a reprimand, and asking them in social situations isn't likely to do your relationship much good either.

Disagreeing before asking questions

When someone gives an opinion with which you disagree and you want to explore your differences, voice your disagreement *after* asking him his reasons for feeling as he does, not before. For example, Alan Garner once met a man who told him that hunting was his favourite sport. Though Alan dislikes the thought of hunting, instead of saying so and letting subsequent questions sound like an inquisition, he asked what the man liked best about it. The discussion gave Alan insights into the challenge the man found in the sport and the vital role he saw hunters like himself playing in the ecological cycle. Alan still does not agree with hunting, but he could see the man's point of view, and this understanding led to a worthwhile conversation and relationship.

Not Being Able to Think of Things to Ask

If you have the opportunity to prepare some questions in advance, you may well have an easier time than if you rely solely upon your ability to think up things to ask on the spur of the moment. Consider the experience of this company executive. 'On Friday, I took a young man named Curtis to a banquet that's held every year to honour new Boy Scouts. Last year's dinner hadn't worked out at all — the scout and I ate our food and sat there in silence. So this year I did some homework. I thought up some questions I'd like to have been asked when I was a Boy Scout — what I'd done to earn a particular merit badge, what practical jokes I'd played or heard about, what types of bridges I'd built and how, what my first hike had been like, what contact I'd had with Girl Scouts. It worked! We had so much to talk about, we didn't want to stop. This simple lesson in a simple social situation was also a valuable business lesson.' So *research in advance* was the key.

The lack of understanding the usefulness of prepared questions in business is often amazing. When you are dealing face-to-face with another person, your success rate in winning him or her over is directly related to whether you are liked as a person. Whether or not people like you is directly related to your ability to ask prepared questions about their number one subject — themselves. There is no such thing as a natural salesperson, negotiator or socialiser. In almost every case, you will find that these are people who have learned the techniques of memorising and asking questions, whether they realise it or not.

You may also find it useful and interesting to memorise some stock questions that you can always use to stimulate conversation. Some surefire conversation starters include:
'If you had to choose another profession (or another job), what would it be and why?'
'If you could spend a week anywhere, where would you choose and what would you do there?'
'How did you get started in that line of business?'

It will require deliberate effort for you to begin asking open-ended questions. Just like walking, writing and all the other skills you've ever learned, after a while you'll be doing it automatically.

Three

How to Start a Conversation

'I decided to marry her. Courtship would be a mere formality. But what to say to begin the courtship?' "Would you like some of my chewing gum?" seemed too low-class. "Hello," was too trite a greeting for my future bride. 'I love you! I am hot with passion!" was too forward. 'I want to make you the mother of my children," seemed a bit premature. So I said nothing. After a while, the bus reached her stop, she got off, and I never saw her again.' End of story.

Starting conversations with strangers is easy, if you know how to go about it. Here are a few simple strategies that we have found useful.

First, seek out people who are likely to be open to talking with you. Most people are delighted to have the opportunity of meeting someone new, and you may consider anyone who is alone and not heavily engrossed in activity to be a good prospect.

Good prospects may show their interest by smiling at you, looking at you more than once or having their arms and legs uncrossed in an open position or their legs crossed towards you, which shows interest non-verbally.

Members of the opposite sex who are attracted to you may indicate this in several additional ways, such as combing their hair, straightening their clothes, rubbing or caressing some part of their bodies or an object like a cup or a chair or letting you catching them looking at you and then holding their gaze an extra second before moving it away.

Once you have decided whom you're going to meet, the next step is to smile, make eye contact, and speak.

Although many people sit around groping for the 'perfect' opener, research has shown that what you say is relatively insignificant. Negative openers, however, won't generally encourage others to talk to you and will probably set a depressed tone for the relationship. A man once approached a woman in a nightclub and said, by way of introduction, 'Boy, I can't stand all this loud music!' She replied, 'Well, then, why don't you leave?'

What you say doesn't have to be wonderfully clever or

dripping with meaning; ordinary comments are just fine. What is important is that you take advantage of opportunities to make contact and get things going. If the other person is interested, he or she will probably give you some free information that will help the two of you find common interests and move the conversation to a more personal level.

Thinking up openers is simple. Basically, you have only three topics to choose from:
- the situation
- the other person
- yourself

and only three ways to begin:
- asking a question
- giving an opinion
- stating a fact

Your major goal in the beginning is just to interest or involve the other person, so the best way to start is usually by asking a question. Closed-ended questions are fine, provided you don't ask too many of them in a row. Stating an opinion also works well, certainly better than just stating a fact. When you recite facts like, 'The bus is late today,' or 'It's a beautiful day', you haven't involved the other person, so he or she is left to try to involve you by asking a question or voicing an opinion, which he or she probably will not do.

Talking about the Situation

Starting a conversation by talking about the situation you are both in is usually the best and easiest of your three options. It's less likely to provoke anxiety than talking about the other person would be, and more likely to promote involvement than talking about yourself.

To begin a conversation about the situation, look around and find things that interest or puzzle you. Use dual perspective: find something to say that the other person is also likely to want to talk about. This is especially easy to do if you are together in a class, on the job, or in a special interest group such as Parents Without Partners, the PTA, Jaycees or Rotary.

After you have asked your question or made your statement, listen carefully for the response. Here are some examples of openers. Keep in mind that they are no better than anything you are likely to come up with, and saying anything is better than saying nothing.

In a sauna: 'Boy, they really stirred up the coals in here! Tell me, what good is this supposed to do?'

At a horse race: 'What do you think will win? Why do you say that?'

At an art gallery: 'What do you suppose the artist wanted to say?' (Alan Garner once spent an hour asking this question in front of a Picasso and got so involved in so many discussions that he accidentally asked someone the same question when he came back for a second look at the painting. His second reply was, 'To tell you the truth, I don't think Picasso has had a whole lot new to say in the past twenty-five minutes.' Then they laughed, Alan disclosed that he was trying out this opener for a new book and so they discussed the book.)

In line for a movie: 'What have you heard about this movie?' 'What made you decide to see it?'

At a market: 'I notice you're buying the artichokes. I've always been curious . . . how do you prepare them?'

To a neighbour: 'Your lawn is green. What's your secret?', 'What's that you're working on?'

In an elevator: 'This must be the world's slowest elevator.' (This may not sound like such a terrific opener, but the other person almost always compares it to one he used to ride in somewhere else — and then that can be discussed.)

At a laundromat: 'What setting should I use?' 'How much detergent should I put in?' (One woman hilariously described the time she added too much detergent and returned later to find an avalanche of suds all over the place! The discussion opened to how many people assume that more is better when it comes to vitamins, which led to swapping experiences with vitamins.)

'Excuse me, where do I put the detergent in?' (While showing this, the woman added that the detergent was much better than what she had used in Hungary, which didn't even remove dirt. This led to an open-ended question about Hungary.)

In a classroom: 'What do you know about the teacher?' 'I was absent yesterday. What did we talk about?' 'What do you think will be in the exam?'

Opening a sale: 'How did you get started in this line of business?'

At a party: 'How did you happen to be at this party?' (Anything is better than 'Haven't I seen you somewhere before?' Allan Pease tried that line many times to test people's response to such a corny statement. The most memorable answer, from a young woman, was, 'Probably — I work at the zoo.')

Talking about the Other Person

Most people like to talk about themselves and will be pleased to respond to any questions or comments about themselves. Before you begin, observe what the other person is doing, wearing, saying and reading, and think of something you'd like to know more about.

At a party: 'That's an interesting jacket. Tell me, what does the insigna stand for?'

In the street: 'You look lost. How can I help?'

At a sports event: 'You're the best player here. What do you do to train?'

After a meeting: 'That was an interesting comment you made to the board. Tell me, why do you think solar energy isn't being developed more quickly?'

To a policeman: 'I'd like to join the force. How do I go about it?'

Meeting someone you have seen before: 'Say, haven't I seen you at a Jaycees meeting? My name's Allan. How did you happen to get involved in Jaycees?'

Passing someone who is walking while you are running around the track or along the shore: 'Want to race?' (The other person will usually laugh. You can then laugh, stop and follow up your remark. If you don't get any response, this is the only opener that allows you to leave immediately!)

While jogging: 'What kind of running shoes are those? Why did you choose that brand?'

At a restaurant: 'Mind if I join you?' (Author Henry Miller never liked eating alone, and often used this opener. Just imagine the hundreds of new people he got to know, people he never would have met had he gone to the nearest vacant table. It's our experience that about 20 per cent of the people you ask will decline, and they will usually apologise, saying they're expecting a friend or have lots of work to do.)

Some psychologists favour opening remarks which directly convey your interest in the other person. For example, 'Hi, you look interesting and I'd like to meet you,' or, 'Hi. I've noticed you here several times and thought I'd come over and introduce myself.' They contend that this method has far more impact on others than do more subtle openers, and that with so many people and stimuli around, it's vital to have impact. The main prerequisite for using this type of approach is courage.

Talking About Yourself

Common as they are, especially amongst lonely people, openers about yourself rarely stimulate conversation. As Dale Carnegie once noted, strangers are far more interested in talking about themselves than in talking about you. Never volunteer information about yourself unless you are asked a specific question. Unless someone asks a question about your family, profession, interests or possessions, they are not interested.

Four

How to Listen Your way to Popularity and Success

'I know you believe you understand what you think I said. But I am not sure you realise that what you heard is not what I meant.'

In conversation, silence is golden because the other person is more interested in himself than in you. He would rather hear himself talk and for you to have a sympathetic ear than anything else, so to win him over you must give him your full attention by listening to him. Every human being has a deep desire to be heard because it makes him feel important and good about himself.

When you become an active listener, you pay the other person a compliment without saying a word. By listening to him talk about something that he feels is interesting, you sell yourself quickly and melt the icicles that often exist on initial meetings.

Active Listening

Active listening is a remarkable way of responding that encourages others to continue speaking, while enabling you to be certain that you understand what they are saying. To use this skill effectively, you need first to grasp what happens when someone speaks with you.

Interpersonal communication begins intrapersonally. Someone has a feeling or idea to express and, in order to convey his message to you, he must first put the message into verbal and non-verbal codes that you will understand. The codes he selects, the words, gestures and tone of voice he uses to convey his meaning, will be determined by his purpose, the situation and his relationship with you, as well as by such factors as his age, status, education, cultural background and emotional state. The process of translating mental ideas and feelings into messages is called 'encoding'.

Suppose, for example, that you are playing a Beatles tape to a friend. He's enjoying the music, but wants it softer. You can't read his mind, so to let you know, he encodes his feelings and shouts above the tape, 'Turn it down!' Once delivered, the message passes through a channel, normally the air space between you. Other sounds in the channel will often distort the message. In this example, the Beatles' loud singing may produce quite a bit of distortion, and the message your ears pick up may be very different from what was sent.

Further distortion inevitably occurs when you decode the message, assigning meaning to the verbal and non-verbal signs you have received. Out of the 40,000 impulses your ears, eyes, hands, toes and the rest of you receive each second, you can only pick out a few on which to focus your attention. What you pick is heavily influenced by such factors as your expectations, needs, beliefs, interests, attitudes, experience and knowledge. According to Sathre, Olson and Whitney in their book *Let's Talk*, 'It has been said that we hear half of what is said, we listen to half of that and we remember half of that.' In other words, we tend to hear what we want to hear and see what we want to see. As Fritz Perls, the founder of the gestalt therapy movement, said, 'The pictures of the world do not enter us automatically, but selectively. We don't see; we look for, search, scan for something. We don't hear all the sounds of the world; we listen.'

For these reasons, the message sent to you is often different from the one you create from the available signs. Your impression often doesn't come close to equalling the other person's intention.

In our Beatles example, if you correctly interpreted the sender's message, you would conclude only that he wanted the music turned lower. But if you interpret it to mean, 'I'm angry at you,' you may well respond inappropriately. Messages are often decoded incorrectly, with neither party ever knowing there has been a misunderstanding.

This is why active listening is so important. Instead of assuming that your impressions are correct and responding accordingly, with this skill you will be able to make certain that you have decoded accurately.

In the example with the loud music, you may reply with, 'You're angry at me, right?'

'No,' the sender would probably reply. 'I just want the music turned down.'

Active listening, then, is telling the sender what his message means to you. It enables the sender to know that you are listening, while enabling you to have your impression either confirmed or clarified.

Here are some other examples of active listening.

SUE: I'll never get a job transfer.
MARIE: You're feeling really frustrated. (*active listening*)
SUE: Yeah. Everywhere I go they tell me to leave a resume, and then they never call me back.
MARIE: You think you're getting the runaround. (*active listening*)
SUE: Exactly. If they haven't got any jobs, why don't they just say so?

HUSBAND: I don't want you to play cards tonight.
WIFE: You don't like me having fun without you. (*active listening*)
HUSBAND: It's not that. It's just that I want to be alone with you tonight.

JUDY: I want to go home.
DAVE: You're not enjoying yourself. (*active listening*)
JUDY: Right. Maybe if the tour guide stopped pushing us around, it would be better.
DAVE: You'd rather he gave us more free time.
JUDY: Yes. I think I'll tell him so right now.

DONNA: We never go anywhere.
JOE: You're bored and want us to take a trip. (*active listening*)
DONNA: Yes. For years we've said we'd go and see the country when we retired. Let's go and do it now!

Active listening once saved a man's relationship with a girlfriend. The third time they got together, while strolling hand-in-hand, he told her how much he looked forward to taking her skiing next winter. She looked away and replied, 'Well, maybe we won't still know each other by then.'

He decoded her message to mean that she didn't want to go on seeing him. But rather than accepting that impression as fact and turning cold towards her (in which case she might have concluded that he was rejecting her), he used active listening. 'Are you saying you don't want to see me any more?' he asked. Her reply was a smile and a hug and, 'No, Jim. That's just my roundabout way of saying that I want you to spend more time with me!'

How and When to use Active Listening

Active listening is very useful in two specific situations:
- When you are not certain you understand what the other person means.
- When an important or emotionally charged message is being sent.

When you employ active listening, concentrate on reflecting the feelings others express, the content, or both, depending upon what you think you might have misunderstood and what you consider most important. To arrive at your statement, ask yourself, 'What is he feeling? What message is he trying to convey?'

In feeding back your conclusion, begin with the word, 'You' and prompt a direct reply by adding at the end, 'Am I right?' In that way, if your conclusion was right you'll know it, and if it wasn't, the sender will clarify exactly what he meant.

Active Listening Demonstrates Your Acceptance

If you were to find yourself in each of these problem situations, which of these three responses do you feel would be most helpful?

A child cuts her finger and begins to cry.

(a) 'That's not such a very big cut.'

(b) 'Stop crying! It doesn't hurt that badly.'

(c) 'Your finger really hurt a lot.'

A close friend confides, 'My boss said I'm not working fast enough and he'll fire me if I don't shape up.'

(a) 'I guess you'd better put your nose to the grindstone.'

(b) 'You shouldn't let him get you down. You can always get another job.'

(c) 'Sounds like your job means a lot to you and you'd hate to lose it.'

A neighbour laments, 'Well, it looks like I've exhausted all my alternatives. I'm going to have to invite my mother to move in with us.'

(a) 'Just look at it this way: your mother brought you up and now you're paying her back.'

(b) 'I'll bet you're secretly pleased to be living with her again.'

(c) 'You're worried about the effect this is going to have on your life.'

The first two responses to each example tell others how they should feel or what they should do, or they express approval or disapproval, sympathy or reassurance. Responses like these seldom help or satisfy those who confide in you. Instead, they generally lead them to conclude that you don't want to get involved, that you don't take their feelings seriously, or that you have little faith in their ability to solve their own problems.

The third response, the active listening response, would have quite another result. Being encouraged to express their emotional reactions fully and freely helps others to become more relaxed and calm around you. Having their problems understood and reflected — but left with them — shows them that you have faith in their ability to arrive at their own solutions. Also, being heard, understood, and accepted without criticism by you will inevitably lead others to feel more positive about themselves, warmer towards you, and more interested in hearing what you have to say.

Many people report major improvements in their relationships with others once they stop judging and begin active listening. One man related his experience. 'When my son used to tell me he had received a bad mark at school I'd ask, "Why didn't you study harder?" When my wife would say she'd been late for work, I'd reply, "You should have left earlier." Once, I recall, my baby daughter told me with tears in her eyes that she was afraid of the dark. I replied, "You shouldn't be. There's nothing to be afraid of." My advice was obvious, but this criticising and moralising was causing my family to confide in me less and less. Last week, my wife mentioned that she had had an argument with her sister. Normally, I would have given her advice such as, "You've only got one sister, so you'd better make up." Instead I replied, "Sounds like you're upset." Each time she spoke I made it a point to only "active listen" — even though I was dying to give her advice. I was thrilled! She shared thoughts and feelings with me that I never knew she had. I felt almost as if I was learning about a stranger. And she seemed delighted by the chance to express herself without being cut off by some glib comment from me.'

Active Listening Keeps your Conversation Going

Active listening is an excellent way of encouraging others to talk to you. The interest you show will frequently lead people to expand upon their comments. The fact that you are not critical of their thoughts and feelings will help you to feel comfortable and to self-disclose more and in greater depth than they otherwise might have done.

Active listening also helps you solve the age-old problem of not having anything to say. If you're frequently tongue-tied, you're probably trying to pay attention to two conversations at once: the one you're having with the other person and the one you're having with yourself. The latter typically consists mostly of worries about your performance. Paradoxically, the more you listen to those worries, the less effective your performance will be.

Active listening encourages you to set aside this troublesome self-talk, to get involved with what others are relating, and to experience what they are feeling. You'll be surprised to find that when you concentrate on your conversational partners rather than on yourself, you will find it far easier to think of things to say. And, since you've paid them such close attention, it will be still more likely that they'll want to hear it.

Common Mistakes in Active Listening

Parroting

Many people new to active listening find themselves merely rewording the remarks of others. For example:

LARRY: I'm having a great time.
TED: You're enjoying yourself.
LARRY: The roller coaster is my favourite ride.
TED: You like the roller coaster best.
LARRY: I hope we don't have to go now.
TED: You want to stay longer.
Parroting responses like these gives the *illusion* of

understanding. Real active listening involves stating your conclusions about the meaning behind what the other person has said.

Ignoring or downplaying feelings

WIFE: I feel like I'm on an endless treadmill, taking care of the kids all day.
HUSBAND: Those kids certainly keep you busy.

MARGARET: I'm depressed.
JANET: You're a little under the weather.

Many people ignore or lessen the intensity of the emotions they hear when they use active listening. It's as though they think that feelings they don't acknowledge will go away. Exactly the opposite is correct. Failing to acknowledge the validity and intensity of the emotions of others tends to increase their intensity, while demonstrating understanding by active listening tends to have a cathartic effect.

Listening too far ahead

You talk at the rate of about 125 words per minute, yet you have the ability to listen at a rate of 400 words per minute, which means that you listen three times faster than you talk. Because of this, the principles of effective listening are sometimes violated by your being too far ahead of the person who is talking, and this can cause your mind to wander. You begin to think about other things rather than listening to the other person, so practise concentrating on *exactly* what the other person is saying.

Active Listening to Non-Verbal Messages

Non-verbal messages are often even more difficult to interpret correctly than verbal messages. This is because the same non-verbal expression, such as a smile or crossed arms, can indicate several widely differing emotions. For this reason, it is often helpful to check out your interpretations through this three-step process.

1. Tell the other person what you saw him do and heard him say that leads you to your conclusion.

2. Tell him what meaning you have tentatively attached to his actions.

3. Ask him if your conclusion is correct.

For example:

1. 'When I asked you to go with me to macrame class, you quietly said, "Sounds like fun," and then changed the topic. I don't think you really want to go. Am I right?'

2. 'You just said you like your job, but you frowned. Would it be right to say there are pluses and minuses to what you're doing?'

3. 'You keep yawning, and I wonder if you wouldn't rather go home. Am I right?'

If you have drawn no conclusions, you may want to state what you have observed and then ask the other person for an explanation. For instance, 'Ever since I met you last month, you've only wanted to get together for lunch—never for dinner or a show. I'm curious to know why that is.' 'When I mentioned skiing in the mountains just now, a little grin came over your face. I'd love to know what you were thinking.'

A friend whom Dave passed in the hallway at work each day suddenly stopped returning his hellos. After this went on for almost a week, he said to her, 'I've been smiling and saying "hello" to you for five days straight and you haven't responded at all. I think I've done something to offend you. Am I right?' She replied. 'No, not at all, Dave. My grandfather died last week and I haven't been able to think about anything else.' Had Dave not used the non-verbal listening technique, he might have done what most people do — silently assumed that she didn't like him and begun to avoid social contact with her.

Non-Verbal Listening to Messages in Business Situations

Negative non-verbal messages are best handled by a non-verbal approach rather than a verbal one. Say, for example, during a negotiation a person sits back and crosses his arms, indicating a potential rejection to your proposition. We know from our research into body language that when a person crosses his arms, his reception and retention of your conversation decreases by about 40 per cent, and that most of his thoughts become negative. Because of this, it is critical in negotiation that you not only read the non-verbal signals but also act on them.

A verbal approach such as, 'I noticed you just crossed your arms. Did I say something you don't like?' may invite an answer like, 'Yes, I don't like your proposal or you!'

Instead, when you decode negative body language in a business situation, use a non-verbal approach to solve the problems. Hand the person something to hold, which will force him to uncross his arms. Body language research shows that unlocking negative body position unlocks a negative attitude and gives you a better chance of getting a positive outcome.

In summary, non-verbal signals in a social situation can best be handled using verbal techniques; in business situations your best strategy is to take non-verbal action.

Additional Listening Rules for Business Situations

In business, your objective is usually to sell yourself first, then your idea, product, service or proposition. In selling, for example, the first stage of the sale is what is commonly called 'the listening step'. Your objective in this step is to ask relevant questions about your prospective customer or his needs and to listen to his answers to try to obtain information that will help you make the sale and to sell yourself as a person to your prospect. Consequently, your ability to listen is directly related to your sales or negotiation success, and our experience shows clearly that that world's best salespeople are also the world's best listeners. Not only must you listen to your prospect, but you often cannot use some of the skills you would normally use in a social situation.

Don't listen with a pencil

Pencil listening is fine if you are at a meeting or attending a lecture or you are expected to take notes. But when you are dealing with people in business, you will break the other person's line of thought by pulling out a pen or pencil and jotting down notes. Not only will the other person consider you impolite, but he may think you are writing down something that he would not want repeated. The best time to take notes is after your business meeting when you are out of the other person's presence.

Faking it

Since you can listen three times faster than you talk, it takes practice to be a conscientious listener, particularly if you are listening to someone who speaks more slowly than you. Think back to the times you have sat, looking the other person in the eye, smiling, nodding your head affirmatively, whilst at the same time thinking about your forthcoming vacation, the grease mark on the other guy's shirt, a party you're going to that evening or your next business appointment. How many times has the other person caught you out by asking 'Well, how do you feel about that?' You've been caught fake listening and your only answer is a bewildered, 'Eh?' Allan Pease was once caught out faking it with a very slow-talking negotiator who said, 'Would you like me to repeat the last bit, Allan?' He replied, 'Which last bit?' He answered, 'The bit after, "Good morning, Allan, nice to see you again"!'

In business your opponent will often give you the benefit of the doubt when he catches you fake listening the first time, but twice is unforgivable. The second time he loses faith and confidence in you.

The danger of fake listening is that you may miss important information that can help you achieve a positive outcome in your favour.

Learning to be an Active Listener

The easiest way to learn the art of active listening is by getting others to paraphrase your remarks. If you want to be certain that someone understands your messages, make them use active listening by saying, 'I want you to listen and tell me what you hear me say. Don't give me your opinion or try to solve my problem. I want to know that you understand me.'

In the emotionally charged atmosphere of arguments, it's easy to misinterpret messages and so active listening is especially valuable. Tell the other person, 'So we'll be certain we understand each other, let's do something new. After each time you speak, I'll tell you what I heard you say before I reply. If I haven't interpreted your words correctly, try again until I do. And you do the same for me. OK?' Then begin the process by speaking and asking the other person what he heard you say or by paying attention, active listening, and then asking if you were accurate.

Be a conscientious listener

Finally, be conscientious in listening to others. Conscientious listening means listening with all your ability. A conscientious listener listens with his eyes and ears, with his mind, with his entire body. When you listen conscientiously, lean forward mentally and physically. Listen intently through the whole conversation. Concentrate on every word the listener says and how he says it. This is the way we learn from others. You will become more popular and have a happier, more successful life.

Five

How to Keep the Conversation Going

The technique of Free Information

'I'll go to Sally's, oh, two or three times a week, or she'll come to see me. We usually talk about our jobs or our kids or some bit of news. I try hard to follow the thread of conversation, but after a while, it's like we've said it all — just ploughed that subject right into the dirt! Then we'll stare at each other or laugh. It sometimes gets kind of embarrassing. Finally, one of us will just make up some excuse to go.'

This woman's experience is quite common — and unnecessary. There's no reason for her, or you, to be at a loss for words. During the course of a conversation, others will almost always be giving you plenty of *free information*, data beyond that which you requested or expected. If you take advantage of this free information by making statements or asking questions relating to it, you'll find plenty of opportunities to channel your conversations in interesting directions.

Consider the following exchanges (with the free information in italics), which are drawn from interactions over a short period of time.

SAM: You certainly dance well, Gloria. Have you had many lessons?

GLORIA: No — this is my first lesson here at Arthur Murray's, but *I used to go out dancing every night when I was living in England.*

ALAN: Hi, Peter, I haven't seen you for ages.

PETER: Yeah, well, *my baby's been sick, so I've had to spend more time at home.*

JOHN: I'm glad to know I'm not the only one who gets most of his news from looking through the papers at news stands.

SHARON: *I'm too busy with charity work* to read much these days.

NICK: Hi, Margaret. Is Laurie around?

MARGARET: No, *he's out buying ingredients for a birthday*

cake we're going to bake.

ALAN: When is the airport bus due?
MAN: It was supposed to be here ten minutes ago. *It's usually pretty much on time.* (*Note:* This sentence, and particularly the word 'usually', is valuable free information because it indicates that the man has frequently taken this bus and that he probably flies often.)

BRIAN: The ocean's certainly acting up today.
AMY: Yeah. *Reminds me of Lake Titicaca during a storm.*

How to take Advantage of Free Information

When you listen closely, you will hear that people are often dropping little pieces of free information like those above.

If you think this free information may be stimulating or useful, that's the time to follow up on it. Not only is it OK to do so, it's the usual method of switching to other topics now and then without worrying whether you ever return to the original topic. Very few social conversations stay on any one topic for more than a few minutes.

To take advantage of free information, make a comment or ask a question about it. As usual, open-ended questions will do the best job of promoting an in-depth response.

GLEN: You have a nice tan, Bill.
BILL: Thanks, Glen. *I got it camping this weekend.*
GLEN: I've never been camping. What do you enjoy most about it?

You may even go back and bring up free information you passed over previously. 'You mentioned earlier that you and Sue were in Fiji last summer. Why did you choose Fiji this time?

Free information also consists of things like the other person's clothing, physical features, behaviour and location. All these can be used as takeoff points for conversation.

'I noticed you have a karate T-shirt on. Do you do karate?'

Sometimes your free information will consist only of a general impression.

'You seem very knowledgeable about South Africa. How do you happen to know so much?'

'You seem more relaxed than when we last met. What's happened?'

'You look like you really enjoy dancing!'

Listening for free information is a valuable skill to keep the conversation interesting, varied and most of all, to keep it going.

Microtechniques

It is frustrating when you think of a brilliant open-ended question to ask and, having asked it, you receive a short answer. For example:

JOHN: How did you happen to move to this area?

FRED: I like the climate better.

At this point you don't have any free information or much else to continue with, so you are forced to ask another open-ended question. For example:

JOHN: What do you like most about this climate?

FRED: It's warmer.

Again, a short answer forces you to think up another open-ended question in an attempt to pry open this hard-nosed clam. The problem is, however, even if you continue to ask good open-ended questions, after a while the conversation begins to sound like an inquisition, with you as the inquisitor.

Bridges

People who give short answers to open-ended questions can be best handled with 'bridges' to bridge their words and keep them talking. Bridges include, 'meaning?'; 'For example?'; 'So then?'; 'Therefore?'; 'Then you?'; 'Which means?'. Each bridge must be followed by silence on your part. Let's take the same conversation between John and Fred, in which John uses bridges to keep Fred talking.

JOHN: How did you happen to move to this area?

FRED: I like the climate better.

JOHN: Better than . . .?

FRED: Better than the polluted air of the city.

JOHN: Which means . . .?

FRED: Which means I can expect better overall health for myself and my family. In fact, I read a report the other day that said . . .

In this case John has not only successfully cracked a tough nut, but he doesn't sound like an investigator. Nor is he doing most of the talking.

To use a bridge successfully, you must do three things.

1. Lean forward, palm out.
2. Stretch the last letter of the bridge.
3. Lean back and stop talking.

Leaning forward with your palm out does two things. First, it non-verbally conveys that you are not threatening in your intent and it tells the listener that it is his turn to talk by non-verbally 'handing over' the control. Stretching the last letter of the bridge converts the bridge to a question, whereas not stretching it can make it sound like a statement. For example:

FRED: . . . and clean air is good for my hay fever.

JOHN: Which meanssssss . . . (*stretched*)

FRED: Which means I should breathe easier. Some people say that it's caused by pollen dust, but I think . . .

Now let's try the same conversation again without stretching the last letter of the bridge.

FRED: . . . and clean air is good for my hay fever.

JOHN: Which means? (*not stretched*)
FRED: Which means mind your own business, big nose!

By not stretching the last syllable of a bridge, you can make it sound like a statement or opinion. It can even sound like an affront, as was the case in the last example.

When you have used the bridge, *stop talking!* Resist the urge to add pearls of wisdom to the seemingly endless silence that can sometimes follow a bridge. The outstretched palm means that the responsibility to speak next has been given to the listener, so let him come up with the next statement. After you have given the control, lean back with your hand on your chin in the evaluation position. This quickly conditions the listener to continue talking for as long as you are leaning back.

Let's listen to an example of a computer salesman using bridges to uncover information from a potential buyer who gave short answers to open-ended questions.

BUYER: We find the Apple computer is very good.
SALESPERSON: (*leaning forward, palm out*) Good? Meaninnnng . . .? (*stretched*)
BUYER: Meaning that it processes the right amount of information. (*short answer*)
SALESPERSON: So thereforrrrre . . .? (*stretched*)
BUYER: We can get the best possible job done at a very economical price. (*longer answer*)
SALESPERSON: Which all meannnnnns . . . (*stretched*)
BUYER: Which means that we look at the efficiency of our equipment, the volume it can produce, and how much operating time it can save us. We relate it to the price, and then make our decision.

By using three bridges consisting of only seven words, the salesperson has opened up a potentially closed customer and has established the criteria upon which the customer will reach a decision.

Bridges are, in effect, shortened versions of open-ended questions. They are best used on people who don't speak much or who give short answers to open-ended questions. First using bridges will feel strange (particularly if you suffer from verbal diarrhoea) because of the silence that sometimes follows a bridge, but if your listener is used to giving short answers, he's also used to experiencing periods of silence during a conversation, so it seems normal to him or her. Bridges are fun to use, they make conversation more productive and give you the power of silent control.

The Head Nod Technique

Nodding the head is a gesture used in most countries to show affirmation. Its origin lies in body lowering or bowing; that is, 'If I bow to you, I am subordinate to you and will do as you command.' Head nodding is, therefore, a shortened or stunted bowing movement.

There are two very useful applications of the head nod technique. Body language, as we shall explore in a later chapter, is an unconscious outward manifestation of inner feelings. If I feel positive or affirmative, my head will begin to make the nodding gesture as I speak. Conversely, if I feel neutral and intentionally start nodding my head, I will begin to experience positive feelings. In other words, positive feelings cause the head to nod — and the reverse is also true; nodding the head causes positive feelings.

Head nodding is also very contagious. If I nod my head at you, you will usually nod, too — even if you don't agree with what I am saying. Many salespeople use this technique to get a customer to agree with them. By finishing each sentence with a verbal affirmation such as, 'Isn't it?', 'Wouldn't you?', 'Isn't that true?', 'Fair enough?', with the salesperson nodding his head, the customer can experience a positive feeling and this creates a greater likelihood of a sale being made. So the head-nodding habit is valuable to acquire in negotiation, selling or persuasion.

The second use of head-nodding is to keep the conversation going. Here's how it's done. After you have asked an open-ended question or used a bridge and the listener gives his answer, nod your head throughout his answer. When he finishes speaking *continue* to nod your head *another five times* at a rate of about one nod per second. Usually, by the time you have counted to four, the listener will begin speaking again and giving you more information. And as long as you remain leaning back with your hand on your chin, there is no pressure on you to speak.

Minimal Encouragers

As the other person speaks, encourage him to keep going by using minimal encouragers. These include 'I see'; 'Uh, huh'; 'Really?'; 'Tell me more'. Minimal encouragers alone can double the length of the other person's statements or information that is given.

Minimal encouragers, combined with the head nod technique and bridges, are some of the most effective tools you can acquire to keep the conversation going.

Six

How to Deliver Sincere Compliments and Honest Positives

'Praise him? I should congratulate that bum for passing PE and English? What about history and science and maths? All Fs: F! F! F! I should say, "Wonderful son! You're well on your way to becoming a garbage man!" No! I just haven't been hard *enough* on him. *That's* the problem!'

Most of us take it for granted when people around us act in ways that please us. Few parents praise their children for eating or playing co-operatively. Few neighbours thank each other for being quiet in the evening.

It's only when others don't act the way we want them to act that we pay them special attention – and quickly! Then we criticise and explain in detail why their behaviour is 'bad' or 'wrong' and why they really should do what we want them to do. Some people scream, threaten and even beat others, to gain compliance.

Reinforced Responses Recur

Ignoring behaviour that you like and punishing behaviour that you don't like is a poor way of helping others learn how you want to be treated.

According to behavioural learning theory, the way others act toward you is determined mainly by how you respond. Actions that you reward will tend to increase in frequency, while actions you ignore will tend to decrease. Actions you punish will decrease, unless the other person is seeking attention, in which case he may continue the behaviour, preferring punishment to no attention at all. Take, for example, the joy with which many children take to swearing once they discover the enormous negative reaction certain words elicit from parents and others.

Behavioural scientists refer to this theory as the three Rs: *reinforced responses recur*. You may find it easier to remember it in diagram form.

Behaviour ———→ Rewarded ———→ Increases
Behaviour ———→ Ignored ———→ Decreases

So, in summary:
• Reward the behaviour that you want continued.

- Avoid punishing the behaviour that you don't like. Many people accept punishment as a reward.
- Ignore the behaviour that you don't want continued. Reward or punishment can both cause an increase in the particular behaviour, whereas ignoring lessens it.

A student of Alan Garner's in Oregon would frequently spot him eating between classes and ask to join him. Shortly after they had exchanged greetings, he would always find some excuse to start complaining about the rain and cold, about the way his ex-wife had treated him, how boring and thankless his job was, or any negative attention-getting statement he could think up. Alan knew he was not having any current emotional difficulties and so he decided to change his behaviour by responding *only* to his occasional cheerful and positive remarks and completely ignoring his negative ones. When he mentioned that a neighbour was helping him fix his car, that an exciting performer was coming to town or that he had run into an old friend, Alan smiled and nodded as he asked him open-ended questions. When he became negative, Alan ignored him. He would look around at a passer-by, start picking the sandwich apart or read the newspaper.

In a short while, the student's behaviour changed completely and he became good-natured and positive around Alan. Every time Alan saw him, he would greet him with a hello and a smile and some good news. Before Alan returned to California, the student confided that those conversations with him were often the best part of his day. This was understandable, because with everyone else he was just as grumpy and negative as ever.

At a San Franciso conversation workshop, after Alan related both this story and the fact that it's more effective to reward behaviour you like than it is to punish behaviour you don't like, two women immediately commented.

MERLE: That really explains a lot. My children haven't been calling me as often as I'd like, so when they do call, I've been very cold and distant-sounding to them. Kind of like Mrs Portnoy in Philip Roth's *Portnoy's Complaint*. 'Alex? Alex?

Do I have a son named Alex? Oh yes, I used to have one, but I haven't heard from him in years.' (laughs) All this has got me a big fat nothing — fewer calls than ever, in fact. Maybe it's time to change my tune.

ANGELA: I help supervise a group of Brownies and we often take them to the country for outdoor activities. The girls constantly seem to tell tales on each other to me, but not to the other adults. I've always wondered, why me? I certainly don't *like* hearing tales. Now I realise that the way I'd been paying attention to their stories, asking questions and working out settlements for all these disputes, had been terrifically rewarding for them! From now on, I think it would be better for me to tell them to settle their own problems.

Not only does it make sense to deliver honest positives in order to encourage others to continue acting the way you want them to act, but it also makes sense because they are more likely to feel good about you.

According to psychologist William James, 'The deepest principle in human nature is the craving to be appreciated.' If you are one of the few people who satisfies this 'craving to be appreciated', you will probably be greatly valued as a friend. Evidence shows that if you compliment others, you are more likely to be seen as sympathetic, understanding and even attractive. In contrast, one study found that couples who stopped complimenting each other began finding each other less attractive. And when others find you expressing your feelings towards them, they are far more likely to open up to you. Thus, with a small amount of effort, you can set up positive exchanges that will help build warmth and intimacy in your relationships.

A final and extremely important reason for delivering positives is that they help to produce an open and supportive climate in which people around you can grow and realise their potential as human beings. Many people wrongly believe that if they express admiration for and acceptance of their children, friends, workmates and spouses, these people will become lazy and begin to rest on their laurels, so their way of encouraging others is to take the attitude that 'enough is never enough' and to endlessly find room for improvement. For example, one particular university student, after slaving for years to do well, was told by his mother, 'You know, I used to think it was a big deal to get a PhD — *until you got it.*'

Considerable psychological evidence suggests that this 'negative' strategy seldom works and is often actually harmful. Rather than continuing to strive endlessly for approval, people who receive only negative feedback generally tend to become exceedingly cautious and self-conscious and begin seeing themselves as inadequate. After a while, they may give up attempting anything. Among those few who are stirred on to great achievement by this strategy, fewer still enjoy their success. Most, echoing critical voices from the past, find something to lament. One such person, who made $150,000 one year by working sixteen-hour days, recently said that, with his brains, he really should have made $300,000. (There was a positive side to this negative statement — it was our first opportunity to meet a person who felt bad about making $150,000 a year!)

How to Deliver Sincere Compliments

The most common way to express admiration is to deliver a direct positive. This type of compliment tells people in a straightforward manner what you appreciate about their *behaviour, appearance* and *possessions.* When we bring up this skill in workshops, we usually begin by asking the participants to compliment us or someone else in the room. Here are some typical compliments in each category.

BEHAVIOUR: You're a good teacher.

APPEARANCE: You have a nice haircut.

POSSESSIONS: I like your shoes.

Compliments like these can be improved with two techniques.

The what/why technique

Most people who attempt to deliver a compliment fail because they tell the other person *what* they like but fail to explain *why* they like it. The power of a compliment depends on its sincerity; only telling a person what you like usually sounds like flattery, which does not work. Never tell a person *what* you like without telling them *why* you like it.
BEHAVIOUR: 'You're a good teacher' can be improved to, 'You're a good teacher *because* you come around and give each of us your personal attention.'
APPEARANCE: 'You have a nice haircut' can be improved to, 'I like your haircut *because* it highlights your eyes.'
POSSESSIONS: 'I like your shoes' can become 'Your shoes are nice because they go well with your suit.'

Saying the person's name

It has been recognised since the time of Plato and Socrates that most people consider their name to be the most beautiful sound in the world and that they pay more attention to sentences in which it appears. In addition, using a person's name is another way of showing that each compliment you pay is tailored uniquely to fit that person. For example:

BEHAVIOUR: '*Alan*, you are a good teacher because you come around and give each of us your personal attention.'

APPEARANCE: '*Sue*, you have a nice haircut because it really highlights your eyes.'

POSSESSIONS: '*John*, your shoes are nice because they go well with your suit.

Research show conclusively that using a person's name causes a greater level of interest in the conversation and, most importantly, the listener will listen intently to the statement that follows his name to see how it will relate to him.

This is a vital point to understand if you are trying to persuade the listener to your point of view. Each time you make an important point, preface it with the listener's name and the attention given to that point and its retention are greatly increased. Become a name user, and others will remember you and what you say for longer.

How to Help Others Accept Your Sincere Compliments

A well-known newspaper columnist received the following letter:

Dear Doris,

My wife has a habit of downgrading sincere compliments. If I say, 'Gee, you look nice in that dress,' her reply is likely to be, 'Do you really think so? It's just a rag my sister gave me.' Or if I tell her she did a great job cleaning up the house, her response might be, 'Well, I guess you haven't seen the kids' room.'

I find it hard to understand why she can't accept a compliment without putting herself down. And it hurts me a little. How do you explain it?

—*Perplexed*

It is likely that you also know many people who have a hard time accepting your sincere compliments. Because of a sense of modesty, a bad self-image or because they cannot think of a way to reply, they often deny the validity of your praise and thereby discourage you from paying them more compliments in the future.

Here are some typical negative responses to our original three compliments.

BEHAVIOUR: Oh, I'm just doing my job.

APPEARANCE: I think the stylist cut it too short, myself.

POSSESSIONS: You like these old shoes?

Whatever the reason for this rejection syndrome, there is something you can do to make compliments easier and more rewarding for you to give and for others to receive. You can follow your compliments with questions. Open-ended questions are best, but anything can work. That way, when others hear your compliments, instead of having to fumble about for a response, they thank you and answer your questions.

Here, then, is what our original compliments look like after using the what/why technique, when the recipient's name is added, and the compliments are followed by a question:

BEHAVIOUR: *Alan*, you're a good teacher because you come around and give us your personal attention. What's the single most common error you can see?

APPEARANCE: *Sue*, I like your haircut because it highlights your eyes. How did you happen to choose that style?

POSSESSIONS: *John*, your shoes are nice because they go well with your suit. What made you decide to go for that style?

This technique takes the pressure off the listener to respond and makes you a pleasant, relaxing person to converse with.

Turning Negatives into Direct Positives

When you set your mind to it, you can almost always find some way to turn destructive criticism into constructive praise. If nothing else, instead of criticising others for failing, you can compliment them for improving in some small way, or for at least trying.

Consider these examples.

Instead of saying . . .	You could say . . .
Too bad you didn't get the rise.	Joyce, I think it's great that you told your boss what you want, even if you didn't get it. What do you suppose you can do next to change his mind?
This story you wrote is ridiculous.	Valerie, I like the paragraph where Burt is being forced to either marry or walk the plank because the adjectives you used make it come alive for me. Where did you get the idea for that scene?
It took you five years to pass the test? What was the problem?	You stuck it out, Bill. Not everyone could have done that. What are you doing to celebrate?
Oops! You bombed out again! Guess you'll have to wait a few more months before you can start again.	Congratulations, Sue. You walked a step farther than you did yesterday!

In cases where someone is doing something you don't like,

you can most effectively encourage a change by rewarding the examples of the behaviour you prefer and by ignoring the behaviour you want discontinued.

Instead of saying . . .	You could say . . .
You left your shirt in the bathroom again. This must be the eleventh time this week I've talked to you about this.	Thanks for putting your stockings in the wash-basket, Laura. Little things you do like that really help me a lot. Tell me what you'd like for dinner tonight and it's yours.
What an idiot! How could you be so stupid as to fail three of your five subjects?	I'm glad you like English, Tony. Your teacher tells me you're especially fond of Alexander Pope. May I see a poem of his you like? (You could also praise whatever effort or progress he makes in the three subjects he failed.)
What do you mean, 'We're going to the show'? Am I some animal you drag around around without even asking what I want to do?	(On another occasion) I'm glad you asked me where I want to go tonight, Don. It makes me feel that my opinion really counts with you.
Boy, your opposition is a long way ahead of you!	I'm really impressed with the way you're working at closing the gap between yourself and your opposition.

If someone never acts in the way you wish, you can praise the behaviour of others who do act in the desired fashion. You can also tell a person what you want and, sometimes, even offer praise in advance for doing it, as illustrated by Melissa's efforts to alter her husband's way of giving her a back massage.

MELISSA: When my husband would push too hard or rub me the wrong way (laughs) — I mean too vigorously — I would put up with it for as long as I could and then angrily shout, 'Stop it!' He would freeze, and it spoiled the mood. Then I tried being positive, saying things like, 'I'd love it if you'd push just a little more gently.' Or, 'That's terrific. Now just a bit lower and more to the right . . . Great!' Not only did I feel good because I started getting what I wanted, he became more confident and spontaneous because he knew he was pleasing me.

How to Make your Sincere Compliments Believable

It is advisable to be honest with your sincere compliments. If the other person even suspects that you're being dishonest, he is less likely to accept future compliments. Also, by being dishonest, you mislead people and increase the frequency of their negative behaviour towards you.

Still, it's not enough to be honest and sincere. If your compliments are to be effective (and affective), the other person has to *believe* that they are honest and sincere. Using the what/why technique, mentioning the other person's name and smiling will certainly help. Compliments will also be more believable if you do the following.

• Start by paying only one compliment every few days to each of your friends and then slowly increase the frequency with which you praise anyone; even one positive remark will receive a great deal of notice.

• Phrase your compliments conservatively at first. Sudden, lavish expressions of appreciation will arouse suspicion. One study suggests that it is best to refer to new acquaintances by name only occasionally.

• Offer positives only when you *don't* want anything. If you tell a workmate how intelligent and creative you find him and then ask for a $20 loan until payday, it's unlikely your praise will be prized.

• Don't always be over-positive; be objective about inconsequential matters. The comments of completely positive people are seldom accorded much credence. For example: 'Thanks for lending me your calculator, Jim. It wasn't easy to figure out how to work it, but once I did, it was a big help in drawing up my estimates. Tell me, what does the sign on this button mean?'

• Don't return the same compliment to others that they have paid to you. For example:

BOB: I like your jacket, Fred.

FRED: I like your jacket, too, Bob.

Praise like this sounds perfunctory, as though it is being voiced merely in order to say something nice in return.

• Don't compliment the obvious; it can make your sincere compliments sound phoney. Let's say you wear a bright red tie to work. It's safe to say most positive compliments you receive that day will be something like, 'Gee, I like your tie'; 'What a beautiful tie'; 'Doesn't your tie look great', and so on. And while you will happily soak up this attention, after a while you will become impervious to any further tie compliments. Everyone compliments the obvious, so avoid it. If someone compliments something obvious like a red tie, take it off and offer to swap it with him. This is the ultimate test of a sincere compliment.

• Favourably compare the person's behaviour, appearance, or possessions to others'. For example: 'Annette, this is the second month running you've been the company's top salesperson. What's your secret?' 'Don, I think you are the fittest member of this club. What do you do to keep in shape?' Compare these for probable impact with 'I like you . . . I like everyone!' On the other hand, you can go overboard with your comparisons. If somebody goes into great detail about why they find you unique, you begin to feel like a freak.

Other Positives You Can Use

Third-person positives

These are compliments intended to ultimately reach someone other than the person you are addressing. You can deliver a third-person positive by telling it to someone within earshot of the person to whom it is intended. Or, you can tell it to someone — a best friend, the local blabbermouth — who is likely to pass it on. Praise delivered publicly in this manner is even more believable and even more valuable than praise delivered privately.

Relayed positives

This compliment involves someone mentioning that he likes the behaviour, appearance, or possessions of another, and you passing on the message. As with direct positives, it's a good idea to follow these up with a question. For example, 'John tells me that you're the best player in the club because you're unbeatable. What's your secret?' A salesperson calling a prospect for an interview could use this compliment which, even though overstated, pays a compliment and makes the prospect laugh. This tension release gives a salesperson a greater chance of securing an interview. For example, on the telephone: 'I hear you're the best accountant in town and I'm ringing to ask, Is that true?'

Indirect positives

With this type of compliment, your words or actions signal

admiration, although that admiration is not expressed directly. For example, when you ask a woman for advice, you are indirectly telling her that you value her judgment. When you ask a man for his name or refer to him by name, you are indirectly signalling that he is significant to you. According to Robert Saudek, who worked with American President John F. Kennedy on the TV series *Profiles in Courage*, Kennedy's manner indirectly conveyed respect: 'He made you think he had nothing else to do except ask you questions and listen — with extraordinary concentration — to your answers. You knew that for the time being he had blotted out both the past and the future.'

How to Receive Compliments

When you start paying others more compliments, you will start receiving more in return. If you want these positive exchanges to continue, it's important that you help those who compliment you to feel good about speaking openly. If you turn away, deny their compliments or change the subject, it's unlikely that this will happen.

On the other hand, if you look a person in the eye and respond positively, he is likely to feel gratified. If he has skilfully followed his compliment with a question, all you need do is smile, thank him and answer. If he hasn't, you can smile, thank him — and perhaps even tell him how you feel about the compliment. Here are some sample responses.

NIGEL: When my wife told me what a good father I am for taking so much time to play with the girls, I hugged her and said, 'I'm glad you see how hard I'm trying. My dad never spent much time with me and I'm making a special effort not to make that mistake.'

KARLA: A neighbour said to me, 'Your car looks nice,' and I replied, 'Thanks, Ann. I washed and waxed it all morning and your noticing makes me feel good!'

MARION: My sister said, 'I love your room. It seems like it would be such a cheerful place to wake up in.' And I replied, 'Thanks, Jan. I designed it with exactly that thought in mind!'

Learning to deliver honest positives and sincere compliments makes good social, personal and business sense. It makes you popular, encourages excellent relationships with others and makes money in business.

Accepting sincere compliments show others that you have a good self-image. Rejecting a sincere compliment is usually interpreted as a personal rejection of the person giving it.

Seven

How To Let Others Know Who You Are

Self-Disclosing

Asking open-ended questions, delivering compliments and paraphrasing will help others to like you and encourage them to let you enter their world. You also need to use the skill of self-disclosing to let them see what your world is like.

The people you meet want to know about you, too: your

attitudes, interests, and values; where you live; what you do for a living; what you do for pleasure; where you've been and where you're going; how available you are for future contact. The information you share provides them with a framework for deciding what type of relationship they may be able to have with you.

If you find that your relationships often die before they really get going, it's likely that you aren't telling others enough about who you are. It's unrealistic to expect strangers to care about you. People only care about those with whom they are involved. And self-disclosure plays a vital role in helping to get them involved.

At best, if you fail to self-disclose, your conversational partners will, for a time, consider you to be mysterious and be intrigued but before long, they'll become frustrated by your lack of reciprocity and will conclude that you aren't interested in getting to know them, are anti-social or have psychological problems.

The Process of Unveiling

Self-disclosure can be a delightful process of mutual self-revelation. The first discloser reveals himself little by little in the hope that when the other person begins seeing him as he is, that person will be encouraged to both learn more and to join in the unveiling.

Self-disclosure is typically symmetrical, meaning that people normally self-disclose at about the same rate as you do. Outside counselling sessions, it's rare for one partner to reveal much more than the other.

You can promote self-disclosure in your relationships by promoting symmetry. Ask questions, show interest in the responses you receive, and then attempt to link those responses to your own knowledge and experiences. Assuming that the other person is not rude or self-centred, he will soon begin asking you questions about your disclosures, too. Here is an example of how this works.

GARY: Hi! Say, aren't you new to this club?

JEAN: Yes, this is only the second time I've been here. I just moved into town.

GARY: I'm new here myself. What brought you to this area?

JEAN: My company moved here from interstate and I'm their chief accountant.

GARY: I have to admire you if you can make a living balancing a company's books. I'm a photographer with the *Daily Sun* and I often have trouble just balancing my own records.

JEAN: A photographer, eh? How'd you get involved in that? You can also promote the process of self-disclosure by modelling the responses you want. For instance, if you want to find out someone's first name, you are most likely to get it by saying. 'By the way, my name's Allan. What's yours?' (If you want the other person's full name, state your full name.) The same is true for addresses, telephone numbers, and any other facts, as well as for opinions and feelings. By being the first to make a revelation, you make it clear that an exchange of information is taking place rather than an interview, and you let the other person know exactly how you want him to answer. Modelling makes it easy for others to reveal themselves.

As self-disclosure proceeds symmetrically and as trust builds, the content of the disclosures typically deepens. Within the course of a conversation, as well as within the course of a relationship, interaction normally becomes more significant and meaningful as it proceeds.

There are four levels through which communication generally passes: clichés, facts, opinions and feelings.

Cliches

When one person encounters another, the two will almost

always begin by exchanging clichés. This ritual serves to acknowledge the presence of another and sometimes to make it clear that each party is receptive to opening the channels of communication to more substantive exchanges.

Typical ritual openings include, 'Hi'; 'How do you do?'; 'Hello. Good to see you.'; 'Pleased to meet you.'

Since these ritual openings are not designed to exchange information, a simple, 'Hi,' or, 'Good to see you, too,' is all that's expected in return.

If you and the other person are heading in the same direction and you aren't interested in discussing anything of substance, you may want to spend the time responding at greater length to his ritual opening or by bringing up insignificant cliché topics such as, 'How do you like this weather?'; 'How are things at work?'; 'How are the kids?'; 'Say, what's happening with your dancing lessons?'; 'What did you think of last night's game?'

Facts

Having exchanged clichés, people generally proceed to exchanging facts. In new relationships, these will usually be the basic facts of your life; in existing relationships, these will typically be recent developments.

'I'm a carpenter in the city.'

'I go windsurfing every Sunday.'

'My aunt's in town and I'm showing her around.'

'Standard Oil decided to send me here for two weeks to get advanced training.'

Early exchanges of facts are very much like job interviews. Each person tries to find out whether there is enough to share to make a relationship worthwhile. This ulterior motive of preliminary conversations becomes apparent in the following conversation.

NEIGHBOUR: Say, Al, do you like tennis? A group of us play every week.

ALLAN: No, I really don't care much for tennis. Do you jog?

NEIGHBOUR: No, but I work out with weights.

ALAN: Well, I'd like to do that sometime, but I'm afraid it might not go well with my martial arts. You don't practise martial arts, do you?

NEIGHBOUR: No.

And so forth. After a while, they smiled and parted with a ritual, 'See you later.' Having found so little to exchange, it's little wonder that neither made any effort to make contact with the other again.

Opinions

'I prefer living in a small town where I know everybody.'

'You should invest in silver if you're really interested in making money.'

'I want to date a lot before I get serious about anyone.'

Opinions give others a more personal insight into you than do facts or clichés. Someone who wants to know what you're really like will come a lot closer by knowing your views on politics, money and love than merely by knowing that you grew up in Sydney and are a librarian.

If you express your opinions in an open-minded manner, you also provide others with material on which to base interesting conversation. On the other hand, if you express your opinions as fact, you will not, as Will Rogers said, 'be leaving a doubt to hang a conversation on'. Everyone approaches reality from a slightly different perspective, and exploring those differences can be both enlightening and exciting.

Feelings

Feelings differ from facts and opinions in that they go beyond describing what happened and how you view what happened; they convey your emotional reaction to what happened. For that reason, your expressions of feeling will generally be considered to give the closest possible insight into who you are. The following example will help make the distinction clear.

Fact: Women are discriminated against for key jobs.

Opinion: Women should be hired on the same basis as men.

Feeling: I felt angry and frustrated when John Roberts was hired instead of me.

Fact: I've been asking at least five open-ended questions a day.

Opinion: Asking open-ended questions has been worth the effort.

Feeling: I'm pleased by the way people have been positive towards me since I've been asking open-ended questions.

Disclosing facts and opinions is important, but if you don't disclose your feelings people begin considering you cold, shallow and uninterested in getting to know them. Also, if you keep your emotions bottled up inside you, you are far more likely to develop a wide variety of physical and emotional illnesses.

Everyone has experienced the sorrow of losing a friend, the excitement of winning, the exhaustion that comes from wrestling with a difficult problem, the soothing warmth of a summer's day, the pain of being alone in a crowd. Everyone hopes to find love, joy and acceptance in her or his life. When you disclose feelings like these to others, you encourage them to identify with you and to share their feelings in turn. Further, by self-disclosing, you avoid the frustrating and self-defeating strategy of hoping others will be considerate of your feelings, even though you have never told them what your feelings are.

How to get others interested in your self-disclosures

Sharing yourself interestingly requires not only that you list facts, but that you tell how you relate to those facts. Alan Garner recalls a man who complained that nobody seemed to be very attentive to anything he had to say about himself. He suggested that they role play a simple situation and see what might be the problem.

'What,' Alan asked him, 'did you do on your last vacation?'

He replied, 'My wife and I drove to Las Vegas and stayed at the Union Plaza and spent a full day gambling. We lost $50 or so between us and had a good time.'

Alan suggested to him that although he had recited the facts of his trip, he hadn't done a good job of self-disclosing. He had talked about the situation, but hadn't talked about himself in the situation, and that's where personal contact comes in. He tried again, this time in writing, with this result.

Sue and I drove to Las Vegas for a taste of big-time gambling. I started out on the 10-cent slot machines, figuring I'd lose $2 or $3 and then stop. After a few minutes, I pulled the lever and became a star! The buzzer went off, red lights flashed, and everyone looked at me and smiled. It was exciting! I was a winner! True, it was only $7.50, but I was so excited it might as well have been a million dollars! I liked the feeling so much that I spent five hours and another $32 making it happen again!

Another woman also had difficulty making others interested in what she had to disclose. Here is how she originally described what she did for a living. 'I'm a bookkeeper for several small companies. I put all their records in order and make sure they pay their taxes correctly.'

After putting herself in the situation, she came up with this description.

I'm an accountant for several small companies. Sometimes when I'm casually writing down figures, I'll start thinking about the thousands of dollars they represent and I'll get nervous in case I make a mistake. When I start feeling that way I go over it one more time, just to make sure.

Sometimes the books I get are really confused — numbers all over the place. Though I grumble a little, I like the challenge of straightening it all out and getting the final figures to match.

Although this is a long-winded job description, writing down your self-disclosures in longhand lets you see how feelings can be expressed. Once you get the hang of it, you can shorten your answers to a single paragraph and still maintain the listeners' attention.

Common Problems with Self-Disclosure

Projecting a false image

If you exaggerate your virtues, conceal your faults, or try to portray your idea of what the other person wants, you decrease your chances for social success and you cause yourself problems.

Projecting a false image will have one of two results.

1. The other person will reject you because he or she is not attracted to the 'perfect' person you are portraying, leading you to wish you had tried to find acceptance as yourself.

2. The other person will be attracted to your lovable act. If this occurs, you won't be able to experience the warmth and acceptance that will be given. The character you are portraying will be receiving it, not you. What's more, you will never be able to relax and be yourself for fear of having your charade uncovered. Almost certainly, the best that can come from this is that you will have to undo your lies.

Consider, for example, this experience.

VICKY: Shortly after I met Don, we talked about children. He said he really loved kids and wanted to have a whole tribe of them. I agreed with his point of view because I thought that's what he wanted to hear, but the truth is that there's no way I want to put up with little brats for the rest of my life. I'm just not the motherly type. After a while we became really close and the next thing I knew, he wanted me to marry him. At that point, I just had to set him straight about children! Unfortunately that ended our relationship. I felt miserable about the whole thing and I still do. I see Don now and then but he avoids me.

IVAN: I challenged George to a game of tennis and introduced myself as a lawyer—it sounds lousy to say I collect money from poker machines for a living. We got together and played a few games during the following few weeks. He even said he was going to introduce me to a gorgeous secretary at his office. One day, George called from jail to say he needed a lawyer and that I was the one he wanted. What could I do? And that, as they say, was that. I've never heard from him again.

When you meet new people, it is wise to be honest and accurate. If a man or woman prefers to be friends with someone richer or more conservative or more interested in stamps or antique cars than you are, that's fine. It's certainly not your fault that you don't fit their bill.

Think of some people you admire and would like to talk with if you could: perhaps Ronald Reagan, Joan Collins, Bob Hawke, Margaret Thatcher, Muhammad Ali, Paul McCartney, John Travolta, Bruce Springsteen or Woody Allen. They are among the most popular men and women in the world, yet none of them comes even remotely close to achieving unanimous approval. Now, if none of them can do it, how can you expect everyone to like you? You can't. It's far wiser to express who you are honestly and let those people who like you become your friends.

Not Being Believed

Self-disclosure will usually help you to have rewarding and intimate relationships, but only if the people to whom you disclose believe you are being truthful. There are three good ways of increasing the chances of being believable.

• *Be specific.* Add names, dates, and places to your disclosures. For example the statement, 'I worked in Europe in 1982,' is less likely to be believed than the more specific, 'I taught English in Malmo, Sweden, during the summer of 1982.'

Instead of describing yourself using general terms like 'tired', 'happy', and 'upset', show how you were feeling by painting word pictures. For example, 'My hands were shaking', 'My knees were knocking'. 'I opened my mouth to scream, but nothing came out', is a lot more believable (and a lot more interesting) that 'I was afraid.'

• *Reveal some negatives.* If you present a balanced picture of yourself, you are more likely to be believed that if you portray yourself in a completely positive light. Your triumphs at work or on the tennis court, for example, will become more plausible if you also relate one or two problems you've encountered.

• *Let them convince you.* If you don't state your opinion immediately, but discuss the pros and cons of the issue with the other person, the conclusion you arrive at is more likely to be taken as being your own.

Not Owning Your Statements

Many people camouflage their expressions of opinion. For example a co-worker once said to Allan Pease, 'You go through day after day at work feeling miserable and you wonder, "Why should you break your back when a big fat nothing is all it gets you?" So before long, you find yourself not really trying. And then they talk about you behind your back.'

It was hard responding to what he had said. He appeared to be talking about himself, but his 'you' statements made it seem that he was talking about Allan. See how much clearer he would have been had he owned his statements by beginning each with 'I': 'I go through day after day at work feeling miserable and I wonder, "Why should I break my back when a big fat nothing is all it gets me?" So before long, I found myself not really trying. And then they talked about me behind my back.'

Another related problem of ownership, which is particularly common among women, is expressing opinions or feelings as questions. If you disguise your beliefs and feelings in metalanguage questions like, 'Don't you think it's getting a little late?' and 'Isn't that awfully expensive?' it's easy for others to dismiss them with such answers as, 'No, we haven't started yet!' and, 'We can afford it.' If you want to be taken seriously, make direct statements and show that you own these statements by using the pronoun 'I,' as in, 'I'm tired and I want to go now', and, 'I don't think we can afford that.'

Holding Back for Fear of Boring the Other Person

If someone is just interested in being amused, a Bill Cosby album or a Woody Allen monologue will do. If someone only wants suspense, an Agatha Christie novel will do. If someone just wants to hear heartwarming stories, James Herriot's *All Things Bright and Beautiful* will do. But people want more than that, and you have something that is far more valuable to them than anything they can get from Bill Cosby, Woody Allen, Agatha Christie or James Herriot. You can give them the gift of personal contact.

Almost everyone in modern society is troubled by the lack of personal contact. Most people have few close friends, many have none at all. Lots of people feel as if they're just being processed all day by teachers or employers, fellow workers, petrol pump attendants or supermarket clerks — often even by the people they live with.

In the light of this, if you can make an honest attempt to establish contact on a personal one-to-one basis, to really touch the other person, your efforts will be welcomed.

Eight

How to Offer Invitations that are Likely to be Accepted

THERAPIST: If you wrote the story of your life, what would you title it?

CLIENT: I don't know . . . How about . . . *Nothing Happened*?

THERAPIST: You mean like that book *Something Happened*?

CLIENT: Yeah. Only 'nothing happened' Most of the time, I feel like a bank guard must feel, like I'm watching everyone, but I'm not really a part of it all — I don't really help shape it. I don't matter to anyone.

THERAPIST: You feel like a spectator watching life go by.

CLIENT: Yeah. Just a spectator. And even when a miracle occurs and I do meet somebody, nothing ever seems to work out.

THERAPIST: You mean you often get rejected?

CLIENT: No. We just talk, then we say goodbye, and that's it.

THERAPIST: You don't invite them to see you again?

CLIENT: No. I think that if they really liked me, they'd do the inviting.

Most people respond to others in reactive ways. They wait for them to make eye contact first, to smile first, to talk first, to issue invitations first. Since most of the people they encounter are also waiting for an invitation, everybody becomes frustrated. Listen to people who typically respond reactively and you'll often hear them passively grumbling about how 'things never seem to work out', when it would be more accurate for them to say, 'I never even try.'

Most men and women who develop successful relationships with others actively work to bring people into their lives. Two of the most important ways they do this are by starting conversations with people they want to meet and by issuing invitations to those they wish to know better. Chapter 3 showed some strategies for starting conversations, and here are some pointers which will greatly increase your chances of having your invitations accepted.

Use Dual Perspective

Different people have different interests. Your invitations are far more likely to be well received and the other person is far more likely to have a good time if you think not only in terms of what *you* would like to do but also in terms of the other person's preferences. Just because you enjoy playing cards, wrestling, or watching romantic 1940s movies doesn't mean that the other person will share your enthusiasm.

It's easy to achieve dual perspective. Ask the other person what activities interest him. Then pick one that would be fun for you too, and ask him to join you.

If you don't use dual perspective in planning your activities, you're more likely to get turned down, and even if you get a 'yes', you may regret it. Some years ago, Alan Garner invited his neighbour, Mario, to go fishing. Alan was so eager to take him that he brushed aside his remark that as a child he had been extremely sick on a boat and ignored his hint that he'd really rather play tennis.

After making his first catch, Mario began to lose colour and complain about feeling dizzy. Although throwing up helped him, he sank to the floor of the boat next to a fish that was flopping about and moaned, 'I told you I get seasick!'

That's what you get when you don't use dual perspective.

Be Direct

It's a good idea to get a firm commitment from the other person before the end of the first meeting. Tell them what activity you have in mind, the day, time and place, and perhaps why you, using dual perspective, think he would have a good time. Then ask if he's interested.

Don't start by asking, 'Are you doing anything Saturday night?' Most people feel embarrassed at responding, 'No, I'm not doing anything at all.' And having said that, some feel resentful at being put into the position of having to agree to your proposal, offer another, or say, in effect, that they'd rather do nothing than be with you.

Start Small

You'd be more likely to lend someone 50 cents than $50, wouldn't you? Well the same is true for other people. The less you ask for, the more likely you are to get it. So if you've just met somebody, he's more likely to agree to a cup of coffee than to a seven-course Chinese dinner.

One of Alan Garner's best friends worked his way into Alan's life by starting small. He phoned him and said, 'Alan, a group of us are getting together at my place for Sunday brunch. We'd like you to join us.' Although Alan didn't think he had much in common with them, he accepted because it didn't sound like a big commitment, it did sound enjoyable, and it wouldn't require much time and effort.

At a sales clinic in England a self-confessed Casanova boldly admitted that his technique for seducing women was to 'think big' and be 'up front' with his approach and so he asked women outright, 'Can I make love to you tonight?' His philosophy was that the law of averages would eventually work in his favour and that 'one in the sack is worth a hundred in the face'.

Using his case as a model, the class decided that his direct approach demanded too much commitment from the listener and suggested that he rephrase his question to ask for a smaller commitment to increase his chances of success.

The new recommended question became: *'Before* I make love to you tonight, would you like to have dinner?' If the woman agreed to the dinner, the major decision was automatically carried. To the class's amazement it didn't work for him. Here's why.

HE: *Before* I make love to you tonight, would you like to have dinner?

SHE: Yes — I would like to have dinner.

HE: Great! What time will you be finished?

Sound Casual

You shape the responses of others more than you realise. If you make your invitations sound like life-and-death issues, they'll be taken as such and you'll be less likely to have them accepted than if you make them sound like a chance to have a good time.

Consider which of these two invitations you would be more likely to accept.

1. A worried expression crosses the other person's face as he looks down, folds his arms on his chest, and says to you gravely, 'I know you're really busy, but . . . I'd like us to get together some time. Maybe if we had the chance, we could become good friends. I wonder if you'd consider playing golf with me Saturday morning.'

2. He looks at you directly and smiles openly as he says in a casual tone, 'I've enjoyed meeting you and maybe we could get together for golf Saturday morning. How about it?'

Research showed that more than 98 per cent of people would accept only the second approach and, of the balance 1 per cent were undertakers and the other 1 per cent were too drunk to answer the question.

If You Get A 'No'

If the other person turns down your invitation, he may not be rejecting you. He may want to get together with you, but may not enjoy the activity you suggested or may already be committed for the time you proposed. If that's the case, he'll usually make the reason clear and you can then make alternative arrangements.

If you are turned down without an explanation, suggest another time or activity, anyway. If the answer is still 'no' and you get no other reassurances, you may decide to conclude that the other person is not interested. Don't ask for a reason; you're unlikely to get the truth and you'll heighten an already tense situation. Instead, exit gracefully by using standard cliches like, 'Sorry you can't make it', or 'Well, I've enjoyed meeting you', or by leaving your number and suggesting he call you at a more opportune time.

Then again, you may decide to persist. A Washington lawyer once read an interview with Alan Garner in the *San Francisco Chronicle* and called to say he'd like to drop by to discuss some of the comments. Alan couldn't make it then, nor any of the next three times he was in town, and he wasn't very encouraging. But the lawyer kept calling and they finally got together six months later in San Diego. Since that time, they have become good friends.

When you get a 'yes'—enjoy it!

Nine

How to Handle Criticism Constructively

No matter how good your relationships with others are, you will occasionally be criticised.

'You're always late.'

'I wish you'd be nicer to my friends.'

'You'll catch a cold if you leave without a jacket.'

'You should come over to see you mother more often. You know, she's not going to be around forever.'

How you handle such critical observations plays a major role in determining the quality of your relationships. If you're typical, you will respond defensively in some of the following ways. First, you may attempt to *avoid* the criticism by ignoring it, by refusing to discuss it, by changing the subject, or by walking away. Here's how Steve provided this post-party dialogue with his wife.

BEVERLEY: Steve, I'm mad at you.

STEVE: Boy, talk about being mad. Just imagine how Mary's husband must feel!

BEVERLEY: That's not what I want to talk about. I want . . .

STEVE: (backing away) Look, I don't know what it is this time, but let's leave it till tomorrow. We've had a good evening and I don't want to spoil it now.

BEVERLEY: (louder) This is important. You made me feel ashamed of you.

STEVE: We'll discuss it in the morning. That's a promise.

BEVERLEY: (shouting as Steve closes the door) Steve!

Someone who criticises you usually wants most of all to have his objections and feelings listened to and taken seriously. When you don't even give him a hearing, you both leave the problem unresolved and compound it by conveying personal disregard. Instead of restoring peace, this strategy typically leads to sharper and sharper outbursts of pent-up tension and to an ever-widening cycle of emotional detachment, as happened with Steve and Beverley.

A second kind of defensive response to criticism is to *deny* it out of hand. Denying it can be just as frustrating and damaging as avoiding it, as you can see in this role play.

VICKI: Allan, I know you've got your heart set on that RX7, but we can't possibly afford it.
ALLAN: The heck we can't! When you want something badly enough, you can always find a way.
VICKI: But the payments are $570 a month! We haven't got that kind of money to spare.
ALLAN: Oh, we'll just juggle the old budget a little.
VICKI: Besides, I've read that the police hate sports cars. If you buy one, they'll probably single you out for tickets . . . and that will be even more expense.
ALLAN: No way. With this baby, I'll be so far ahead of them, they'll never catch me!

At the end of this interchange, Vicki said that she thought her objections had received no consideration whatsoever. She said she felt so frustrated and angry that she wanted to scream just to make Allan listen. Had this been a real dialogue, their relationship would probably have suffered and Allan would have denied himself any real benefits that might have come from taking Vicki's advice into account.

Third, you may attempt to *excuse* your behaviour by explaining it in detail and downplaying its importance. Here are some fairly typical examples supplied by students.

NANCY: You were supposed to call me yesterday.
GRANT: Gosh, I'm sorry. Some of the switchboard clerks were on strike and I had to fill in. I can't tell you how hectic it was. By the time I got off work, I was just too tired.
NANCY: So you left me hanging around, expecting a call that wasn't coming?
GRANT: Oh, you're always so busy, I bet it was no big deal, and I'm furious!

FATHER: How can you spend $3,000 for a vacation in France?
JUDY: Dad, $3,000 isn't so much any more. Besides, I'm old enough . . .

FATHER: Old enough to know better. That kind of money is enough for you to pay your grocery bills for a year, or to finish university.

JUDY: Dad, I'm going to finish university. I've only got a year to go, and I know I will. This just isn't the time.

FATHER: And when the time comes, you'll be too broke to do it. Then you'll come to me again.

JUDY: That was just a five-day loan till pay day. I paid you back, didn't I?

FATHER: Yes, you did, but it says something. It says that you live on the edge of poverty! You never save anything for a rainy day.

JUDY: (quietly) It's hard to save.

FATHER: Especially when you blow three thousand bucks for ten days of pleasure. And you'll be there all alone!

JUDY: I can take care of myself. All year long I've been cooped up in my office and I just want to spread my wings and experience life a little.

FATHER: The way you're going about it, the only thing you'll be experiencing for some time will be trouble.

Excuse-making puts you in a distinctly one-down position. Your one-up critic, having failed to receive even acknowledgment that his feelings or reasons have really registered, usually gets increasingly angry while labouring to counter each of your excuses with reasons of his own. Frequently, this defensive technique causes minor disagreements to snowball into full-fledged arguments.

A fourth defence is to respond to criticism by striking back, 'fighting fire with fire'. Here are some examples.

GAY: Carol, your clothes don't look too good today.

CAROL: *You* should talk after wearing that jumpsuit to the party last week! That was ridiculous!

TOM: Janice, you should have been ready earlier. Now we'll be late for the show.

JANICE: Oh, well, look at Mr Perfection. I suppose you don't remember all the times *you've* kept *me* waiting!

Striking back is a very tempting response. Your critic who, after all, isn't perfect himself, has both attacked you or your behaviour and provided you with an excuse for releasing your tension back at him. However, though it may be temporarily satisfying, striking back usually causes great harm to relationships. It hardly ever leads to any consideration of the real problems or to possible compromises. Furthermore, it promotes heated arguments and causes people to lose respect for each other: 'I try to reason with him, but all he does is yell. I don't think he has a brain in his head,' and to lose respect for themselves. 'Why did I tell her that? Now she'll really think I don't care about her. How dumb of me!'

Since the typical defensive ways of responding to criticism fail to achieve anything positive, let's consider an honest and constructive alternative. Assertively practising the following alternative will help you to realise that you don't have to become defensive when others point out what *they* consider to be your mistakes. Further, it will enable you to gain valuable insight into their thinking. Finally, you can pacify your critics by allowing them to see that you are taking their opinions into consideration, even when you don't agree with them.

A Constructive Alternative

Step 1: Ask for details

This alternative involves two steps, the first of which is to *asks for details*. Criticism is often given in generalities. 'I don't like your attitude,'; 'You don't care about me'. Requesting particulars will enable you to find out exactly what the other person's objections are. This skill is neither an offensive weapon nor a defensive shield: it is a tool for understanding.

It's simple to *asks for details*. Like a reporter, all you do is pose questions designed to find out who, what, when, where, why, and how.

Whom did I embarrass?

What do I do that leads you to say I don't care?

When did I ignore you?

Where did I make a fool of myself?

Why do you feel that I should stay home more?

How do I act when you say I turn you off?

In helping the other person to clarify his remarks you may want to *asks for details* by suggesting possible complaints and asking whether they are a problem. And, since your goal is understanding, once you find out, you may even want to ask whether he has any additional complaints to make. Since most people who criticise you probably expect you to respond defensively, make sure your voice carries no hint of sarcasm.

Here are some examples that further illustrate how this skill works.

SON: You don't care about me.

FATHER: Why do you say that? (*asks for details*)

SON: You'd be nicer to me if you did.

FATHER: What would you like me to do? (*asks for details*)

SON: (*silence*)

FATHER: Do you feel that I don't care about you because I didn't let you bring your friend to the soccer games with us? (*asks for details*)

SON: No.

FATHER: Is it because I didn't buy you a bag of lollies? (*asks for details*)

SON: Yeah. All the other kids got to eat ice-cream and lollies and I didn't.

MANDY: Boy, are you a cheapskate!

TOM: What's wrong? Didn't I tip the waitress enough? (*asks for details*)

MANDY: No, it's not that.

TOM: Do you think I should have called us a cab? (*asks for details*)

MANDY: Well, it is shaping up to be an awfully long walk.

In our seminars, we often have an exercise in which participants are invited to point out some real or imagined shortcoming that we have while we *ask for details*. Here's how one such exercise went.

VAL: I don't like a lot of things about you. (*smiles*)

ALAN: Could you be more specific? (*asks for details*)

VAL: Your clothing.

ALAN: Is it my socks, my shoes, my shirt, or my trousers? (*asks for details*)

VAL: I like tight trousers better.

ALAN: Anything else? (*asks for details*)

VAL: No, everything else is OK.

ALAN: How about the colour of my trousers? Is that OK? (*asks for details*)

VAL: Yes, I like it.

MICHAEL: There's something about the way you conduct this workshop that I don't like.

ALAN: Uh-huh. What do I *do* that you don't like? (*asks for details*)

MICHAEL: The material — it's all useful, but there's a lot to learn.

ALAN: Are you saying you wish I'd cut down on the number of skills I teach? Or maybe that you wish the class was longer? (*asks for details*)

MICHAEL: No, I just wish you'd go a little slower, add a few more examples, and allow a bit more time for practice.

Using this skill encouraged these participants to respond in greater depth and to examine their own thinking. Although further questioning revealed that Val's objections were given in jest, Michael's were genuine. It was only because Alan was able to *ask for details* that he learned this valuable information. Had Alan changed the subject, explained why he taught the class as he did, or told Michael the real problem was that he was slow, Alan never would have received the benefit of Michael's valuable insight.

It's especially useful to *ask for details* when you think your critic may have an ulterior motive, as in the following dialogue.

BOB: Hello.
CHARLIE: Hi, Bob. What you doing?
BOB: Hi, Charlie. I'm right in the middle of watching the grand final. The Tigers are ahead by two goals.
CHARLIE: Are you really wasting this beautiful afternoon watching football?
BOB: What is there about my watching football that you don't like? (*asks for details*)
CHARLIE: Nothing, Bob. I just thought you might want to get in some tennis.

Bob's use of this skill rapidly ended Charlie's attempt at manipulation. Rather than getting enmeshed in an argument about the merits of football or of watching TV in the afternoon, it allowed Bob to find out quickly what was really on Charlie's mind. Charlie benefited because this technique made it easy for him to say what he really wanted. It also allowed him to examine his right — wrong structure to see whether he really feels it's wrong to watch TV on a Saturday afternoon.

Occasionally, when you *ask for details*, you will find that what you thought was criticism really isn't. Once, Alan Garner delivered a lecture to a class at the University of Oregon on Plato's view of the nature of reality. The talk was well received, and so he was surprised later when a friend said, 'Why are you still wasting your time with Plato?'

He was tempted to strike back and inquire how she, a

physical education major who whiles away much of her life playing badminton, could have the nerve to criticise him for his interest in Plato. Instead, he asked, 'Why do you think Plato is a waste of time?' To his surprise, she replied, 'I just think your real talent lies in psychology and in teaching people to excel!'

Step 2: Agree with the criticism

After you *ask for details* and find out exactly what the other person's objections are, the next step is simply to *agree with the criticism*.

But how can you agree with criticism that is plainly wrong? Simple. There are two types of agreement statement, and you can always use one or the other while at the same time maintaining your own position. Here are your options.

Agree with the truth

If you listen non-defensively to your critics, you will frequently find yourself agreeing that much of what they have to say is valid, accurate or likely in your opinion, to happen. When this is the case, your most powerful response is to *agree with the truth*.

Consider these examples and note how the person being criticised agrees with the truth. The defensive remarks that could have been made are in italics.

WIFE: You got sand in our camera when you took it to the river.

HUSBAND: You're right. Next time I'll keep it inside a paper bag. (*Next time, don't ask me to bring it. I'm going for a walk!*)

JOHN: You certainly didn't do a very good job of negotiating that turn.

KATHY: I agree, I did turn too sharply. I'll try to slow down before turning next time. (*I did the best I could with this old car!*)

HOWARD: You always want to go to the movies.
SUE: That's true. I do like to go at least once a week. (*And you always want to play cards!*)

HELEN: I don't think you should quit your job. You've got seniority; if business turns bad, you'll be the last to go. On any new job, you'd be the first.
KEN: Good point. Maybe I should think about this a bit more. (*What do you know about the working world? You've never had a job!*)

MOTHER: If you go out dancing tonight, you'll be tired in the morning.
DAUGHTER: I probably will, but it's worth it to me. (*You never want me to have any fun!*)

KERRY: That apartment may be beautiful, but it's thirty kilometres further away from work. If we move in there, we won't see each other as much, and our marriage is likely to suffer.
MARK: That's a real possibility, though I'd love to live in the country. (*Look, there are talkers and there are doers. Let's be doers!*)

You will note that although everyone in these examples *agreed with the truth*, no one put himself or herself down. Instead, they assumed what Thomas Harris calls an 'I'm OK, you're OK' position *vis à vis* their critics. By contrast, avoiding the issue and excusing their behaviour would have put them in an 'I'm not OK — you're OK' position; striking back would have put them in an 'I'm OK — you're not OK' position.
By practising this response, you will soon feel more comfortable in situations that formerly left you or your critics upset.
   It's simple to learn to agree with the truth. The first step is to think about whether the criticism directed at you is accurate or likely, in your estimation, to come to pass. If you

have frequently received the same criticism, you may wish to look particularly closely for evidence to back up those objections. (When you agree with criticism, you can most effectively acknowledge your agreement by repeating the key words used by your critic; 'You're going to be late.' 'That's true, I most likely am going to be late.'; 'You didn't clean up your room.' 'You're right. I didn't clean up my room.' This does a far better job of showing your critic that he has been heard than does just saying, 'Yes', or 'That's right.')

If you intend to change in response to the criticism, *agreeing with the truth* and then stating what you expect to do differently will normally restore harmony. Even if you don't intend to change, you will improve the situation by assertively saying so after *agreeing with the truth* and admitting that your behaviour may be a problem for the other person. Your critic will be satisfied that the problem has at least been acknowledged and will probably respect you for being so forthright. Certainly, he will like you better than if you had *agreed*, pretended you were going to work on the problem, and then carried on as before.

Often, criticism will be delivered to you in uncategorical terms, using words like 'always' or 'never' to describe your behaviour: 'You're always late,'; 'You never ask for my opinion'; or labelling you: 'You're stupid (a failure, slow, selfish)'. When you are confronted with criticism that is obviously too broad, you can agree with the part that you think is true and disagree with the rest. Citing proof will most effectively help you to back up your disagreements.

These interchanges occurred during a communication workshop.
EDDIE: You're always late.
ALLEN: I certainly am late today, though I've been early every other day this month.

CAMERON: Your company gives lousy service.
ROBERT: We were slow for a short while, that's true, and now we are really sharp.

HARRY: You certainly are a slow eater.
SANDRA: I am eating rather slowly tonight, though last time we went out I finished before you.

JERRY: You blew that big sale. What a failure you are!
DAVID: Well, in this instance I certainly did fail, but I made five pretty big sales last week.

Notice that several of these responses are affirmative self-statements in disagreeing with criticism. Affirming your abilities and past successes helps build your self-confidence and helps others see that you have a positive self-image.

The significance of making positive self-statements is shown in this interaction between two men jogging.
BILL: You're only running five kilometres? I'm shooting for ten.
RAY: Sixteen kilometres is farther than three, and I think both of us are doing pretty well.

Contrast this last response with the message Ray might have sent to Bill. 'I guess my five kilometres is *nothing* compared to what you're doing.')

Sometimes, critics will cite general truths to make you agree to do what they wish. Even here, it's completely possible for you to agree with the truth yet still to reject your critics' conclusions.

You may agree with the general truth, for example, that it's important to save for your old age. But it does not necessarily follow that you can't ever buy a nice new outfit, eat out, see a first-run movie or go away from home on holidays. You may agree that it's important to help your fellow men and women, but must you therefore give to your critic's favourite charity? Ridiculous! You would lead an absurd and miserable life indeed if you always tried to follow all the general truths you believe. Besides, general truths frequently contradict one another; a stitch in time may save nine but, then again, haste makes waste.

Given these facts, when somebody cites in general truth, you can quite legitimately *agree with the truth* while maintaining your position. Consider these dialogues:

GALE: Put down your work for an hour or two and let's go swimming. You need exercise to keep healthy.
BOB: I agree that I need exercise to keep healthy, but I've got to defend a client in court tomorrow, so I can't swim today. (*Agrees with the truth and self-discloses*)

RHONDA: What do you mean you're not going to help me collect for the Red Cross? You know, each of us has to chip in if we're going to help the underprivileged.
JAN: I agree that we all need to do our part, but I wouldn't feel comfortable collecting money at someone's door. (*Agrees with the truth and self-discloses*)

MOTHER: You really should give up selling used cars and get a job with a regular income. Too much pressure isn't good for you.
SON: You're right in saying too much pressure isn't good, Mum. But I'm enjoying my job and I plan to keep it. (*Agrees with the truth and self-discloses*)

In these sample interchanges, Bob, Jan, and the son not only agree with the general truth, they also *self-disclose*. They don't provide long, involved justifications for their behaviour but they do choose to explain it. Imagine what might happen to Bob's friendship with Gale if he didn't *self-disclose* and frequently had dialogues like this.

GALE: Put down your work for an hour or two and let's go swimming. You need exercise to keep healthy.
BOB: I agree that I need exercise to keep healthy, but no thanks. (*Agrees with the truth*)
GALE: What do you mean, 'No, thanks'? Are you busy? Do I have bad breath? What?
BOB: Just no thanks.

If the other person is being manipulative, if you really don't want to explain your reasons or if your reasons are based upon your physical or emotional state, you may wish to follow Jan's example and *agree* and *self-disclose your feelings*. Disclosing feelings is an excellent strategy; it leaves the other person with little to counter, since feelings afford slim grounds for argument. Rhonda could say to Jan that Jan shouldn't feel the way she does, but then Jan could counter, 'You may be right, but I do.'

Agree with your critic's right to an opinion

You will often disagree with your critics' predictions about the consequences of your behaviour.

'If you go out walking tonight, you'll probably get mugged.'
'If you keep spending so much on clothes, you'll wind up in the poorhouse.'
'You're going to get fat, eating so much spaghetti.'

You can't be absolutely sure that you won't be mugged, wind up in the poorhouse or get fat. Nothing in life is certain, and critics often turn out to be correct.

Since you can't be certain that criticism will always prove to be inaccurate even when you disagree with it, you can certainly *agree with the critics' right to an opinion*. Doing so will help you to give some thought to differing points of view, while at the same time helping you maintain your own position. Neither you nor your critic need be branded as 'wrong' or 'not OK'; you are simply two people who see an issue differently. Consider these examples.

DOUG: If you buy silver now, you'll lose your shirt. Silver is due for another big plunge.
LYNN: Silver could nosedive, but its industrial use is so great that it's just bound to skyrocket in the long run. (*Agrees with the critic's right to an opinion and self-discloses*)

JANE: Maybe you should call off the wedding. With the divorce rate the way it is, you're almost bound to fail.

MERLE: I respect your opinion, Jane, but I think if I work hard at it I can make this marriage work. (*Agrees with the critic's right to an opinion and self-discloses*)

Critics will often present you with value judgments as though they were truths, and your most constructive response, once again, is to *agree with the critic's right to an opinion.* For example:

CAROL: How can you read such a trashy magazine? Why not read Shakespeare, Dumas, or at least Steinbeck, for a change?

JUDY: I can see why you might think that *Mad* magazine is a bit gross, Carol, but I think it's funny. (*Agrees with the critic's right to an opinion and self-discloses*)

SARAH: I think you should quit your job. With your education, you could do a lot better.

REBECCA: Thanks for the compliment. Not too many cocktail waitresses have graduated from college and it's easy for me to see why you think I could do better. But I like the hours — and the money. (*Agrees with the critic's right to an opinion and self-discloses*)

DAN: How can you buy a Datsun? Don't you know that a Toyota is a much better car?

SANDY: Toyotas certainly have sleek lines and good mileage. But I like the handling of a Datsun better. (*Agrees with the critics right to an opinion and self-discloses*)

When you totally disagree with criticism, you may wish to voice the disagreement. But then again you can usually find some way to *agree* with it while affirming what you believe to be the truth.

PATIENT: I don't think you're really a doctor. You look much too young.

DOCTOR: Thanks. You're not the first to say that, and it's true that I haven't any grey hair or lines on my face. All I can say is I am a doctor. (*Agrees with the critic's right to an opinion and self-discloses*)

ANGELA: No butter for me, Pat. I'm on a diet.

PAT: Ha! I've heard you tell me that one before!

ANGELA: You're right in saying that I've failed in the past and I can't blame you for not taking me seriously now. But this time I'm getting a dietician's help and I *am* going to make it! (*Agrees with the critic's right to an opinion and self-discloses.*)

Bringing Your Skills Together: Two Sample Dialogues

Dialogue 1

MARIE: I don't really believe that you'll leave your job at the bank to sell encyclopedias.

PETER: Why do you say that, Marie? (*Asks for details*)

MARIE: Well, for one thing the bank offers a regular salary.

PETER: That's true. (*Agrees with the truth*)

MARIE: And besides, you're not the salesman type.

PETER: What do I do that leads you to think I'm not the 'salesman type'? (*Asks for details*)

MARIE: You're not pushy enough.

PETER: Your opinion is understandable, Marie. I think that not being very pushy is my best asset for selling. (*Agrees with critic's right to an opinion and self-discloses*)

MARIE: If you didn't make any sales one week, you wouldn't eat!

PETER: You're right, I wouldn't (*Agrees with the truth.*)

MARIE: And, anyway, most people who start out selling encyclopedias don't succeed.

PETER: You're right in saying that it's a tough job and the majority don't make it. I'm certainly glad to be in the minority group who do. (*Agrees with critic's right to an opinion and self-discloses*)

Dialogue 2

FATHER: Steve, your mother and I don't want you to move out.

STEVE: What don't you like about my moving away? (*Asks for details*)

FATHER: That . . . that apartment of yours. It's a *lot* smaller than our home. Why, you could fit the whole thing into your room here at home.

STEVE: That's true. What is it about its size that bothers you? (*Agrees with the truth and asks for details*)

FATHER: For heaven's sake, Steve, you'll be sleeping in the same bedroom with your roommate, what's his name?

STEVE: Doug. That's true. What is there about our sharing the bedroom that you don't like? (*Agrees with the truth and asks for details*)

FATHER: Look, Steve. I know you're not a fairy and your mother knows you're not a fairy, but Doug has a reputation of being, well . . . effeminate. What will your neighbours think?

STEVE: I don't know. It doesn't really matter to me. (*Self-discloses*)

FATHER: They'll think you're gay — that's what they'll think!

STEVE: You may be right. (*Agrees with the critic's right to an opinion*)

FATHER: Why do you want to live there?

STEVE: I think I'll enjoy living near the ocean. And I want to become a little more independent. (*Self-discloses.*)

FATHER: Steve, you're hurting your mother and thumbing your nose at everything we've built.

STEVE: Dad, I can see how you might think that. A lot of people my age do blindly rebel against their parents. But that's not the case with me. (*Agrees with the critic's right to an opinion and self-discloses.*)

Handling Criticism in Business

When a client, customer or potential customer criticises you or your organisation the 'put the boot on his foot' technique is extremely useful and can be a lifesaver. When you receive a criticism you ask your client or customer what *he* would say or do if *he* were in your position and received that same criticism. For example, this dialogue between a potential customer and a sales representative.

Dialogue 1

CUSTOMER: I've heard your delivery time is terrible.

SALESMAN: Yes, it's true we were pretty slow at one stage. Tell me, if you were the manager of a company that received comments like yours, what would you do? (*agrees with critic's right to an opinion and puts the boot on his foot*)

CUSTOMER: I'd reorganise my warehouse and couriers so that deliveries were on time!

SALESMAN: That's right. That's what we did!

The salesman has not only agreed with the truth but said that his company had already taken the customer's advice. Where does the customer go next with his criticism? Nowhere. When you ask the customer what he would do, you then say, 'That's what we did'. If, in fact, your company hasn't done it, you don't deserve the business.

Dialogue 2

CLIENT: I wouldn't deal with your company because the last guy who called to see us was a rude, arrogant slob!
PUBLIC RELATIONS MAN: I can understand your feeling like that. Tell me, if you were the manager of a company and client said that to you, what would you do? (*agrees with critic's right to an opinion and puts the boot on his foot*)
CLIENT: I'd stop that person from dealing with clients and relocate him to another job.
PUBLIC RELATIONS MAN: That's right. That's what we did!

Again the PR man agrees with the critic's right to an opinion and tells him that the company has taken his advice.

This technique can also be used at the wrong time. Take this example.
IRATE CUSTOMER: Any company who employs a stupid sales manager like yours doesn't deserve my business.
PUBLIC RELATIONS MAN: I can understand your saying that. Tell me, if you were the manager of a company and a customer said that to you about the sales manager, what would you do? (*agrees with the critic's right to an opinion and puts the boot on his foot*)
IRATE CUSTOMER: I'd fire the sales manager!
PUBLIC RELATIONS MAN (without thinking): That's what we did!

The skills and philosophy behind handling criticism constructively are designed to allow you to handle problems and people from the same side of the desk. It avoids the usual confrontations and angry scenes, and it's fun. Like any new skill it takes practice and repetition to make them conditioned responses and an integral part of your conversational technique.

Ten

How to Resist Attempts at Being Manipulated

Relatives, friends, neighbours, co-workers and even strangers will occasionally try to make you do things you don't want to do by asking you over and over again, giving you lots of attractive reasons, and criticising you for refusing. They believe that if they try hard enough and long enough, they will wear you down and win you over. If you give in, you're likely to feel angry at the other person and disgusted with yourself.

Fortunately, there is an easy-to-learn technique that will enable you to outlast even the most persistent manipulative attempt. It's called 'broken record' because it requires that you, like a broken record, repeat the same words over and over.

The three steps that precede your using 'broken record' are the same that you can use in handling criticism. First, if you don't understand the other person, ask for details. Second, once they are clear, agree with the truth or agree with the critic's right to an opinion. Third, self-disclose the fact that you don't want to do what is being asked of you.

Having done that, if the other person persists, use 'broken record' by continuing to agree with whatever he says while repeating over and over, using the same words, the fact that you don't want to do it. No one can argue with a broken record and so your would-be manipulator will usually give up.

The following sample dialogues illustrate how to use this valuable skill.

Dialogue 1

STAN: Uh . . . hello, Genevieve.
GEN: Hi, Stan. What's new?
STAN: Well, Gen, I'm here to give you a chance to help your fellow man. (*Uses a cliché*)
GEN: Really. How can I do that? (*Asks for details*)
STAN: Well, as you know, I collect for the United Fund every year.
GEN: Wait a minute, Stan, and I'll get my purse.
STAN: Genevieve, I need a little more help this year. I'm going to be away on vacation during the collection drive.
GEN: Oh, that's too bad, Stan.
STAN: You could do a good turn and really help me out of a jam if you'd collect from the neighbours in my place.

GEN: Gee Stan, you're right in saying it would be a good turn and it would help you out, but I'd rather not collect from the neighbours. (*Agrees with the truth and self-discloses*)

STAN: And it would give you an opportunity to keep in touch with Meg, Liz and Veronica and all your other friends. Besides, you said you wanted to meet more people in the neighbourhood. Well, Gen, here's your chance!

GEN: Yes, Stan, it would be a good opportunity to see my friends and meet new neighbours, but I'd rather not collect from the neighbours. (*Agrees with the truth and uses broken record*)

STAN: I'm sure you'd be very good at it. Everyone in the neighbourhood likes you.

GEN: It's nice of you to say that, but I'd rather not collect from the neighbours. (*Broken record*)

STAN: You know, of course, that it would only take an hour of your time.

GEN: I'm sure it would only take an hour, Stan, but I'd rather not collect from the neighbours. (*Agrees with the truth and uses broken record*)

STAN: You know, the United Fund does a lot of good for people in disasters like those floods in Victoria — and even when the dam broke in Western Australia.

GEN: They certainly do, but I'd rather not collect from the neighbours. (*Agrees with the truth and uses broken record.*)

STAN: Why don't you want to do it, Genevieve? I don't understand.

GEN: I know it may not make sense to you, but I'd rather not. (*Agrees with the critic's right to an opinion and uses broken record*)

STAN: It doesn't sound like you care all that much for your fellow man, Genevieve.

GEN: I can see how you might think that, but I'd rather not collect from the neighbours. (*Agrees with the critic's right to an opinion and uses broken record*)

STAN: I don't think you're going to do this little favour for me.

GEN: You're right Stan, I'm not. (*Agrees with the truth*)

Dialogue 2

GARY: Hi, Bill! How are you? (*Ritual opening*)
BILL: Fine. Yourself? (*Ritual opening*)
GARY: Good. And how's your Rolls? (*Smiles*)
BILL: Oh, it's fine too. (*Laughs*)
GARY: Say Bill, my relatives are flying in from interstate tonight.
BILL: That's good news!
GARY: And if I drive up in your Rolls Royce, man, what an impression I'd make on them!
BILL: I'm sure you would make quite an impression, but I want to drive the Rolls myself tonight. (*Agrees with the truth and self-discloses*)
GARY: Well, hey, why don't you drive my car tonight?
BILL: Yes I could do that Gary, but I want to drive the Rolls tonight. (*Agrees with the truth and broken record*)
GARY: Listen, Bill. Isn't this type of thing that friends are for? I mean friends *should* help each other out.
BILL: I agree that friends should help each other, but I want to drive the Rolls tonight. (*Agrees with the truth and broken record*)
GARY: Where are you going that's so important?
BILL: I'm taking Margie to see a movie. (*Self-discloses*)
GARY: I'm sure she wouldn't mind if you drove my car.
BILL: Yes that's possible, Gary, but I want to drive the Rolls tonight. (*Agrees with the critic's right to an opinion and uses broken record*)
GARY: Bill, it's not as if you haven't lent me your car before.
BILL: That's true, but I . . . (*Agrees with the truth*)
GARY: And haven't I always returned it to you in tiptop shape? The last time I even cleaned and polished it and filled up the tank before I brought it back. Why, I even vacuumed the carpet and emptied the ashtrays.
BILL: (*Laughs*) You certainly did do a good job of taking care of my car and you are welcome to have it some other time. But I want to drive it tonight. (*Agrees with the truth, self-*

discloses, and broken record)
GARY: Well, how about Thursday? I'll be taking them out to dinner, and your car would really set the mood.
BILL: I won't need it on Thursday, Gary, so it's all yours. *(Self-discloses)*

Dialogue 3

ERICA: Well, Bernie, where shall we eat tonight?
BERNIE: I don't know. There's a new Mexican restaurant opening up in town. Why don't we try it out?
ERICA: Anything but that, Bernie. Mexican food is just too fattening and I'm going to stick to my diet. *(Self-discloses)*
BERNIE: Yeah, but Mexican food is so good.
ERICA: It really is good, but I'm going to stick to my diet. *(Agrees with the truth and broken record.)* How about Japanese?
BERNIE: Look, one day off your diet won't kill you.
ERICA: I agree that it won't, but I'm going to stick to it. *(Agrees with the truth and broken record)* Why don't we try a vegetarian restaurant?
BERNIE: In fact, I think it would be psychologically healthy for you to loosen up a little, Erica.
ERICA: I can understand your saying that, Bernie, but I really want to lose this weight, so I'm going to stick to my diet. *(Agrees with the critic's right to an opinion, self-discloses and uses broken record)* Japanese would be really nice.
BERNIE: Erica, *nobody* sticks to *any* diet. It's just a matter of time before you give in. So why not give in now?
ERICA: True, most people do give up, but I won't. I'm going to stick to my diet. *(Agrees with the truth and uses broken record)*
BERNIE: OK, OK. You want the truth? I'll tell you the truth. I got an introductory coupon for this Mexican restaurant — two for the price of one! — and it expires tonight! If we don't use it now, I might as well throw it out.

ERICA: I can see that it will cost extra, Bernie, and you will miss out on this good deal, but I'm going to stick to my diet. (*Agrees with the truth and uses broken record*)

BERNIE: All right, how about pizza? I hear they have a Tuesday night special: all you can eat for $3!

Like Genevieve, Bill and Erica, when you use 'broken record', you'll be able to hold off even the most persistent manipulative attempts.

Eleven

Body Language: How to Read Others' Attitudes by their Gestures

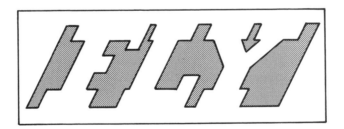

Look at the above illustration. What do you see? Most people see a number of irregular solid shapes but to the trained eye the word 'FLY' appears. Did you unconsciously focus on the solid shapes? Most people do. With face-to-face communication, most people hear mainly what is said and miss the non-verbal signals that are as obvious as 'FLY' becomes in the illustration when you focus your eyes on the white segments.

A New Science

Ever since Allan Pease put pen to paper on *Body Language— How to Read Other's Thoughts by Their Gestures* in 1976, people everywhere have been pulling, scratching, rubbing, tugging, adjusting, twitching and squirming. The book, which is an international bestseller, has become part of most sales and people management training courses and has been set for courses in universities and colleges. On a professional level he has been involved with interpretation of and for politicians, police, doctors, dentists, salespeople, judges, lawyers, interviewers, actors, TV personalities, psychologists, psychiatrists, and even convicted murderers, all over the world. Body language is not new — it is the original signalling system that was used in the pre-verbal era and was recorded in art form on the cave walls over one million years ago. It wasn't until the middle of the last century that Charles Darwin documented his observations of body language in *The Expression of the Emotions in Man and Animals* that any real scientific progress began. Sigmund Freud was among the first to use body language as a tool in understanding his patients, Ray Birdwhistell carried out extensive studies in the 1950s, Desmond Morris brought it to the public in the late 1960s. Allan Pease and others established its use in the business arena during the 1970s and today it has become a valuable business skill.

So what makes this science of body language or kinesics so popular and intriguing? It is because we know from research that in a face-to-face encounter non-verbal signals account for 60 to 80 per cent of the impact of your message on your listener. This means that most of what you communicate to your listener is done without opening your mouth. When you know what to look for and how to decode what you see, you have a powerful tool for understanding others and knowing where you stand with them.

A Message from the Unconscious

The subtitle of this chapter, 'How to Read Others' Attitudes By Their Gestures' is not a technically correct statement. Body language becomes an unconscious message sent from the brain that becomes an outward reflection of a person's emotional state, that is, it is a reflection of how a person *feels*. Having assessed how the person feels, you match those feelings with what the person says with consideration to the *context* and *circumstances* in which he or she said it, and you can arrive at a reasonably accurate analysis of what they are thinking. This is easier said than done, as face-to-face encounters are highly complex events. Slow-motion video replay is excellent for increasing your body language awareness.

Who Reads It?

Tests conducted with babies under six months old and their parents show interesting results. Video clips of the babies crying were shown to each mother and, with the sound turned off, the mothers were asked to determine the baby's need. Most mothers could accurately distinguish pain, tiredness, wet pants, hunger, the need for attention and a range of other emotions. Most fathers, however, could see only a crying baby, highlighting the fact that women are excellent readers of non-verbal signals and men are comparatively poor. If the female of most species of animal did not have this innate ability to decode the signals of its young, it would be detrimental to the survival of that species. What we usually describe as gut feeling, hunches, sixth sense and women's intuition often refers to the unconscious ability to read body signals and decode them. So bad luck, fellas. If you are going to lie to your wife or lady friend, we suggest you do it in a letter or get a friend to do it over the telephone. Face-to-face lying to a woman rarely succeeds.

The Impact of Body Language

The 1960 US Presidential debate between Kennedy and Nixon highlights the impact of body language, because the majority of those who *heard* the debate or *read* the transcripts felt that Nixon had performed better than Kennedy. The majority of those who *saw* the debate on television, however, felt that Kennedy was by far the better performer. Same information, same two people – the body language performance of Kennedy was the factor that made the difference.

Australian Lindy Chamberlain received massive publicity over the mysterious disappearance of her nine-week-old baby Azaria on a camping trip to central Australia in 1980. She claimed that the baby had been taken by a wild dog, but the authorities were trying to prove she had killed her. Throughout the trial, Mrs Chamberlain appeared on TV and in newspaper photographs with an emotionless facial expression. The Australian public, women particularly, decoded this expression as guilt, even before the trial began. When Mrs Chamberlain approached Allan to ask if he could attend her trial to decode the body language of certain people, he was amazed to find a smiling, friendly, and emotive person, remarkably different to the one projected through the media. She told Allan that she had been instructed by her advisors to keep a neutral, unemotional facial expression and to suppress her habitual nervous laugh, which had previously been interpreted in isolation and out of context, much to her detriment. Unfortunately for her, this emotionless appearance caused overwhelming public hatred towards her. Similarly, Bruno Hauptmann, the alleged kidnapper of air ace Charles Lindbergh's child, forfeited public sympathy because he displayed no emotion during his trial.

The point here is not whether they were innocent or guilty but it demonstrates that, as in the Nixon-Kennedy debate, people make the decisions about others based on what they see — if you project body language signals that do not reflect the real you, you will be judged by others on what they *see*. Mrs Chamberlain was subsequently convicted of murder on circumstantial evidence and sentenced to life imprisonment.

Clusters of Gestures

The question most often asked about body language is something like this: 'What does it mean when someone rubs his nose? Is he lying?' The answer is a definite maybe! It could also mean that he has an itchy nose, bad breath, new false teeth, has not shaved that day or had garlic for lunch. It could

Figure 1   *Lying cluster*

also mean that the person *is* lying, as nose touching is one of the gestures commonly used to signal deceit.

Like most other languages, body language consists of words, phrases, expressions and punctuation. One word alone can have several different meanings. Take for example, the word 'dressing'. It can mean the act of putting on clothing; that with which something is dressed; a sauce for food; stuffing for a fowl; an application for a wound; fertiliser for land or the grooming of a horse. To try to interpret 'dressing' in isolation from other words is futile. If 'dressing' is put into a sentence with other words it can be understood; for example, 'After my shower I began dressing myself'. Here you can understand the exact meaning of the word 'dressing' in relation to the other words around it.

The same principle applies to understanding body language. You cannot take one gesture or signal in isolation and try to interpret its meaning. You must look at a body language 'sentence' called a *cluster* to arrive at a correct interpretation. Let's say for example, that a woman asks me how I like the new dress she is wearing. Now, I am experienced and polite enough to realise that there is only one answer to that question, 'I like it,' even when I don't. Let's say that I answered the question with, 'I love it. You look beautiful, and I noticed you when you first walked in.' If this was the truth, and there is no metalanguage in the sentence to suggest it is not, I would probably have had my palms visible as I made the statement, indicating that it is a truthful statement. But what would it mean if, at the end of the statement, I briskly rubbed my nose nine or ten times? It would probably indicate that I had an itchy nose. How would she feel if I replied to her question this way? 'Frankly, I love it (*nose touch*). It makes you look beautiful (*eye rub, looking down*) and I noticed it when you first walked in (*tugging at collar*).' In this case, the body language is in a cluster and is in context to the words. To the trained eye, it clearly signals that I'm lying, whereas in the first example I had an itchy nose. Notice also that the second example is laced with metalanguage, confirming that

I lied. *Frankly* signals lack of frankness, *it makes you look beautiful* says that *you* are not beautiful and only a dress can make you appear beautiful, and *I noticed it* confirms that I didn't notice you, I noticed your dress instead, probably because it looks so bad.

Everybody has one or more repetitive gestures that signal boredom or tension. Nose touching, hair twirling, ring fiddling or collar pulling are common examples; because an individual uses one frequently, you notice it. These repetitive signals are often seen in high-tension situations such as waiting for the dentist, being in the casualty ward of a hospital or being a first-time air traveller. They are indicators of stress, occurring repetitively in isolation of other gestures, and out of context to verbal sentences. Never take one gesture or signal in isolation and interpret it. Look for gesture clusters and you will be amazed at how often you can read a person's true feelings.

Gestures in Context

You also need to take into consideration the context in which gestures occur before reaching a conclusion. We know, for example, that when people feel *defensive*, which generally means negative, insecure or even hostile, they often fold their arms across their chest. This is sometimes reinforced by crossed legs or ankles and negative facial expressions. Now look at the woman in Figure 2. How does she feel? Is she negative? Defensive? Insecure? If she had just been insulted, we could safely assume that her gestures were in context and signalled defensiveness. But what if she is enjoying social conversation and has merely had too much to drink and needs to go to the bathroom? Notice how one leg is pressed firmly over the other in a 'holding back' position. It is very likely that she needs to go to the bathroom.

Figure 2 *Is she cold or does she need to go to the bathroom?*

Contrast this position with the woman in Figure 3. Here is a gesture cluster which would occur if the woman felt defensive. If she was standing with strangers we could assume that, in context, she felt unsure of other people. If the conversation was pro-communist and she was pro-capitalist, it would show that she was rejecting the conversation. It would also show that she had a closed mind. If she needed to go

Figure 3   *At first glance she appears relaxed but the gestures reveal tension*

to the bathroom or felt cold, she would be more likely to be standing like the woman in Figure 2. Always consider gestures in context and in clusters before reaching a conclusion.

Cultural Differences

As words change from culture to culture, so the meanings behind gestures can change. Frequent travellers are aware of this and sometimes they learn the different meanings the hard way. For example, look at the gesture in Figure 4. What does

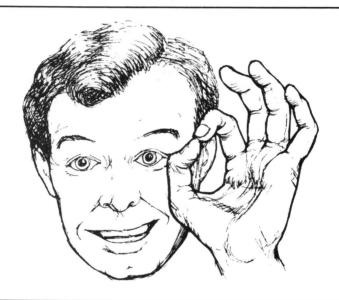

Figure 4   *Don't show this to a Maltese*

this sign mean to you? If you are an English-speaking Caucasian it means 'OK', 'good' or 'spot on'. If you are French, it could mean 'zero' or 'worthless', and a Japanese would read it as 'money'. How about its meaning to a northern Greek or Maltese? In those countries it is used as a sexual insult, that is, to imply that someone is like an orifice (or words to that effect) or as a signal that a man is homosexual. Consequently, if you, as an English-speaking Caucasian, use this sign in northern Greece or Malta to tell a person that he is 'OK' he would be insulted, and might retaliate. (Alternatively, he may invite you home for an intimate dinner for two.)

The gesture in Figure 5 is also commonly misinterpreted. To English-speaking Caucasians, it is an 'OK' signal. To most Europeans it signals the number 1, as they count from 1 to 5 beginning with the thumb for 1 and ending with the little

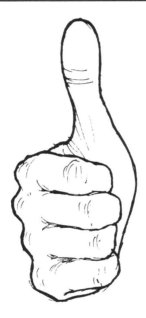

Figure 5 *In Greece this will get you into trouble*

finger at number 5. Westerners usually start counting on the index finger for number 1 and end on the thumb for number 5. But what does the thumb-up signal mean to a northern Greek? Again, it is an insult signal meaning 'get stuffed' (or similar expression). British or Australian hitchhikers can never understand why this signal doesn't invite a Greek motorist to stop and give them a ride.

Understanding a person's cultural upbringing helps avoid misinterpretation of gestures and misunderstanding of someone's intentions or feelings. Most Europeans stand closer in social conversations than do Australians, Americans or English. Consequently, Westerners call Europeans 'pushy' and Europeans call Westerners 'standoffish'. Asians will not look a Westerner in the eyes, as it is a cultural sign of disrespect, so the Westerners misinterpret the Asians' intentions as 'shifty'. Danes hold a gaze longer than do the English in social situations, so the English call the Danes 'rude' or 'starers' and the Danes refer to the English as 'cold' or 'unfriendly' through what the Danes interpret as *lack* of eye contact.

In these examples there are no right or wrong signals, only cultural definitions. When you know what to look for, encounters with other cultures become fascinating and fun. Lack of cultural understanding is a major contribution to disharmony between different races.

Gestures and Meaning

The remainder of this chapter shows how basic emotional states relate to body language. We have shown eighteen basic emotional attitudes and the gestures that most often occur to reveal these attitudes. This chapter is intended as a general reference to body language and has therefore been simplified for quick reference. Although we have presented each gesture in a freeze-frame, be mindful of the three rules of body language interpretation — clusters, context and culture. The emotional attitudes we will examine are:

boredom	defensiveness	deciding
evaluation: critical	expectancy	concealment
evaluation: positive	uncertainty	readiness
superiority	empathy	frustration
confidence	equality	disapproval
openness	dominance	disbelief

Boredom

To the extent that the hand acts as a support for the head, the person is proportionately bored — the more the support the greater the degree of boredom. In Figure 6, the listener

Figure 6 *Total boredom*

is very uninterested in the speaker and little more explanation is needed. There are however, greater and lesser degrees of hand-to-head support. When a person's head is completely supported by the hand and he is making loud snoring sounds, you may safely assume that he is not interested. Hand-to-head support signals are also present in the critical evaluation gesture.

Figure 7   *Having negative thoughts*

Evaluation: Critical

It is rare that someone using this gesture cluster is experiencing anything other than critical thoughts. If you are a speaker, it is probably the most disconcerting position you can see your listener take. The longer he stays in the position, the more critical his attitude becomes. This gesture is usually part of the critical evaluation cluster seen in Figure 8. He has an arm barrier and leg cross (defensive), head down (disapproval), body turned away (non-involved), leaning back (lack of interest), lowered left eybrow (critical) and constricted pupils (negative), to name a few of his characteristics. To convince this person of anything is usually futile. Your best approach is to hand him something to alter his position.

Figure 8 *You won't convince this man of anything*

Evaluation: Positive

Contrast the above positions with Figure 9. You will notice that in this gesture the hand rests against the cheek or face and is not acting as a support. This position is taken by a person who is evaluating positively or objectively what he is hearing and is considering the pros and cons of the situation. This positive gesture cluster also includes a slight head tilt (interest), leaning forward (interest) and dilated pupils (interest).

Figure 9   *Tell me more . . .*

Figure 10   *Superiority—maybe one day you'll be as smart as I am!*

Superiority

We called this the 'lawyer's position' as it is the trademark of most members of the legal or accounting professions. It is the position most favoured by managers, people in authority or those who feel that they are smarter, wiser, better or generally superior to their listener. It is also the favourite position of wise guys, smart alecs, know-it-alls and power players. Lawyers and the like do it at each other to show that each is as knowledgeable as the other and it is a constant source of agitation when the boss does it to a subordinate or when a man does it to a woman. To combat this gesture, copy it. Don't copy your boss if he does it to you, however, or you may suddenly find yourself unemployed. (fig. 10)

Confidence

The steeple gesture (Figure 11) is one of the few gestures that can be interpreted in isolation of the other gestures and has

Figure 11 *In poker, he's just been dealt a good hand*

one specific emotional meaning — confidence. The man in Figure 11 has either just picked up four kings in a game of poker or feels the chess piece you are moving is to his advantage or likes the solution you are suggesting, is confident about what he is saying or is in a situation in which he may feel confident. The steeple is a dead giveaway to his confident attitude. Women usually steeple on their laps, which is less aggressive than the raised version that men use.

Openness

The open palm gesture can be traced back to Stone Age drawings and was used to indicate that a person had no weapons held or concealed. Today it has evolved as a gesture

Figure 12 *An openness display*

showing openness, honesty or submission. Someone being completely frank or open with you will intuitively use his or her palms while speaking. Someone who is not open or honest will intuitively put the palms out of sight in pockets or under the arms. Have you ever noticed where a child puts his hands when he lies? He puts them behind his back and out of your sight. Open palms are the key to detecting an honest, open attitude. Liars almost always hide their hands when lying.

Defensiveness

Crossing the arms on the chest is a universal gesture signifying a closed mind; its probable origin is protection of the heart and lungs from attack. Those who are habitual arm crossers

Figure 13   *Turned off*

disagree with this, claiming that they are 'comfortable'. This is also true. People who have a closed, reserved or defensive attitude always feel 'comfortable' in this position. Any gesture feels comfortable when you have the corresponding attitude.

Figure 14   *A negative approach*

If you are among strangers, this position will feel comfortable. If you are with your best friends having a good time, it feels uncomfortable. The man in Figure 14 is sitting in a typical full defensive gesture clusture with crossed arms and legs, clenched fists (hostile) leaning back (non-participative) head down (critical) coat buttoned (protective). We cannot decode any eye signals because of his sunglasses and his upper lip and face are bearded, which prevent us from decoding facial expressions. All of these factors make it almost impossible for a person who presents like this to establish any credibility or rapport with strangers.

Expectancy

We rub our palms together when we are expecting a result. Fast rubbing showing excited expectancy and slow rubbing shows expected benefits for the person who is rubbing his palms. 'Let me show you this great deal,' says the con man, while slowly rubbing his palms together. 'Let's go to the

Figure 15   *'Let's get started.'*

movies!' yells the excited child whilst rubbing his palms quickly, showing his enthusiastic expectancy of the event. The speed of the palm rub is the key to who is to receive the benefits.

Uncertainty

Scratching the neck below or behind the ear is the usual sign that a person does not understand your message. When the person says, 'I don't understand what you mean' the neck-

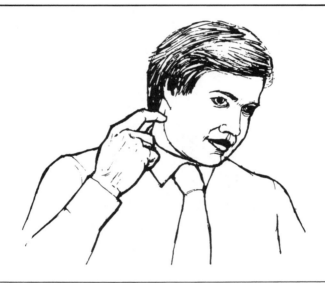

Figure 16   *He doesn't understand*

scratching gesture confirms the verbal message. But what about the person who says 'Yes, I understand', while using the same gesture? When the verbal and non-verbal channels are in conflict, the non-verbal is the most reliable guide to how the person feels. Scratching the top or back of the head can also show uncertainty (in addition to dandruff).

Figure 17   *Mirroring to show empathy*

Empathy

Look at the two men in Figure 17. Are they friends or strangers? How can you tell? When two or more people have a 'rapport', we mean that they have a mental alignment with each other. The visible body language signs of this mental rapport are mirror images of gestures. That is, we copy and mirror the gestures of people whom we like. To build a rapport with you, I need only copy your gestures and body position for you to begin to feel that I 'understand' you. Studies show that when we are among strangers, we avoid taking in mirrored positions.

Equality

The origin of the modern Western handshake is in the ancient ritual of arm wrestling, where the winner would finish with his palm on top of the loser's. Hence the expression 'the upper hand'. The modern handshake is a horizontal version of arm wrestling. The person whose hand is more 'upper' than the

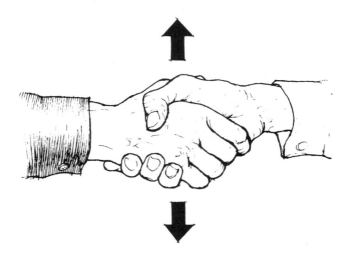

Figure 18   *The equal handshake*

other person's has 'the upper hand' and assumes a dominant role. When the other person resists his palm being turned over, the result is a firm grip in which the contestants are 'equal'. It is a 'draw' and each person feels 'OK' about the other. Historically, the leaders of most groups who engaged in arm wrestling were male, resulting in the fact that shaking hands with women is still relatively new, particularly in Australia and New Zealand, where female hand shaking is still an awkward, even embarrassing event for most men.

Dominance

For obvious reasons, this position is popular with dominant males. They usually slip discreetly into this position and, when the opportunity presents itself, they attempt to dominate the

Figure 19 *A favourite of the dominant male*

listener, the group or the conversation. The easiest way to handle the notorious chair straddler is to give him a chair with arms on it. Another trademark of the dominant individual is the palm-down shake, in which their hand is on top of yours (Figure 20). An easy way to neutralise this aggressive handshake is give him a double-handed handshake that sandwiches his hand between yours.

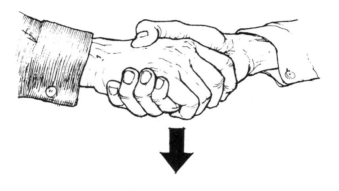

Figure 20   *Getting 'the upper hand'*

Deciding

Ask a group of men and women to consider two alternative solutions, A and B. Tell them to take 60 seconds to think it over and you see that the majority will begin to stroke their chins (Figures 21 and 22). This gesture shows that an internal decision is taking place and your best approach is to remain silent until the chin stroking ceases. Often the gestures that follow indicate whether the decision is positive or negative.

Figure 21   *Reaching a decision*

Figure 22   *'What should I do?'*

Concealment

Research conducted with people in occupations who, by definition, were classed as professional liars — nurses, actors, politicians and lawyers — showed interesting results. In one series of tests, nurses were instructed to lie to patients about their health and to be convincing. In the next series of tests, the nurses were instructed to be completely open and honest with patients about their health. Video replay revealed that when the nurses were truthful they rarely touched their faces. If they did touch their faces it was usually in isolation of other gestures or out of context. When the nurses lied, however, their hand-to-face touching frequency increased up to ten times the norm. Put simply, people who lie usually start touching their faces and heads. The nose touching gesture (Figure 23)

Figure 23 *Lying through his teeth*

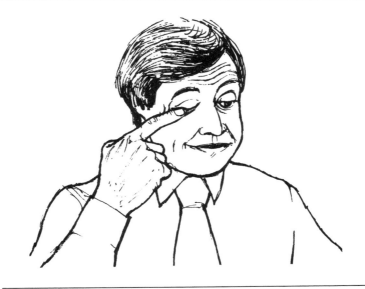

Figure 24 *'I can't see it'*

probably has its origin in mouth covering to hold back deceitful words. Eye rubbing (Figure 24) has its origin in a child covering his eyes with both hands to avoid looking at an unpleasant event or person. The person who 'can't really see it' will often use this signal. (Women rub below their eyes to avoid smudging their make-up.)

Readiness

Just as most birds, fish and animals fluff, puff or blow themselves up to appear larger for courtship or aggression rituals, so humans perform similar actions in the same circumstances. Hands on hips can make you seem wider and rocking up and down on the soles of your feet make you appear taller. The question is, what is the person ready for? The circumstance in which the gesture occurs is the key. He could be ready to argue or ready to depart, ready to punch

Figure 25 *Ready for action*

you in the mouth or ready to ask you for a dance. The man
in Figure 26 is demonstrating seated readiness. In context, he
could be ready to leave, ready to participate or ready to buy.
The prevailing circumstances are the key.

Figure 26 *Seated readiness*

Frustration

When someone is telling you an untruth and they get the feeling that you suspect the lie, they will often use the collar-pull gesture, which can give the game away. It is almost as if the person is letting air circulate around his neck to cool it down. Motorists caught in heavy traffic use this gesture to signal their frustration at the situation. Rubbing the neck is

Figure 27 *'Was I speeding, officer?'*

also a frustration signal. Whenever two dogs become angry at one another, the hair on the back of their necks stands on end and sweating occurs on the skin's surface. The same condition occurs when a human being experiences a person or event that makes him uptight, frustrated or even hostile. To satisfy this tingling feeling caused on the neck by this reaction, he begins rubbing the back of his neck; hence the expression 'a pain in the neck'. Imagine the person in Figure 27 using this gesture whilst telling you how wonderful it is to see you again.

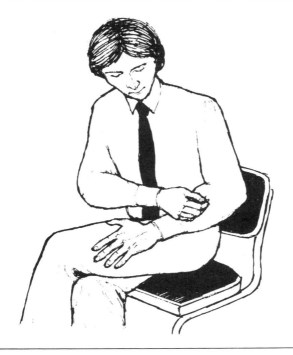

Figure 28 *A disapproving attitude*

Disapproval

Have you ever noticed the person who picks imaginary pieces of lint or fluff from his clothing as you are giving your opinion on something? What you are observing is a clear signal of lack of interest or disapproval. A person who is being shown a friend's family movies of little Johnny at the beach uses it to signal lack of interest, but put a sixty-year-old person with a group of teenagers discussing the virtues of smoking marijuana and the sixty-year-old will use the imaginary lint-pick gesture to unconsciously reveal disapproval. Its use is a way of avoiding the speaker's eyes so as not to reveal one's own feelings or opinions. Likewise the disapproving cigarette smoker averts his eyes, usually downwards, and exhales the smoke in a downward direction. Blowing the smoke down almost always shows a negative attitude. It was the signal favoured by actor Humphrey Bogart whenever he played a suspicious or secretive character.

Figure 29   *Disapproving and negative*

Disbelief

When a child tells a lie, he will often cover his mouth with his hand in a subconscious attempt to stop the deceitful words from coming out. When an adult wants to suppress his words

Figure 30 *Restraining his words*

or opinions, he will often do a similar thing. There is nothing more disconcerting than an audience that sits like this when you are giving your opinion. People who do not believe or agree with the speaker use this gesture and it is a visible indication that they are withholding their words. If a child doesn't want to hear his parents' reprimands, he may cover his ears with his hands. The adult versions of this include tugging the ear lobe, screwing the finger in the ear or bending the ear forward to cover the earhole. It is a gesture usually indicating, 'I've heard enough'. Imagine the person in Figure 31 saying, 'That sounds *really* interesting' as you recount the time you bought a 1923 sixpenny Queen Victoria for your stamp collection.

Figure 31 *He's heard enough*

Courtship

While courtship gestures and rituals could fill a book (and probably will soon) we will examine a typical social scene, starring one lucky man and two eager women, using gestures that most of us use or decode without awareness. Both women are using classic courtship clusters. Let's take the woman on the left. 1. Shoe balancing on top of foot with foot and toes thrusting in and out of the shoe (*phallic*). 2. Legs crossed toward the man (*interest*). 3. Sitting close (*territorial advance*). 4. Holding wrists back to give display (*ancient erotic ritual*). 5. Head tilted (*interest*). 6. Pupils dilated (*excitement/interest*). 7. Hair fondling (*preening*). 8. Chest protruding (*attention-getter*). 9. Smiling; teeth visible (*submissive*).

In addition to these signals, you will also find that she exhales the cigarette smoke in an upward direction (*confident*).

Next, the woman on the right. 1. Sitting on leg, knee pointing towards the man (*courtship*). 2. Hand caressing thigh (*desire to be touched*). 3. Exaggerated head tilt (*competing with other woman*). 4. Whole body pointing at male (*attempting to capture attention*). She also has exposed wrists, dilated pupils, teeth visible, chest out and looking over her rounded shoulder (*breast mimic*).

Figure 32 *Who will be his choice?*

Now to the lucky fellow in the centre. He probably has a 'gut feeling' that things are going well. He is unconsciously responding to these displays with: 1. Tie adjusting (*preening*). 2. Legs spread (*crotch display*). 3. Chest out, shoulders back (*size display*). Notice also that the lower half of his body leans towards one woman and the top half toward the other woman so that both women can savour his magnificent body (*chauvinist thinking*).

This scene is a frozen piece of time during a courtship ritual; minutes later more signals will be added and others eliminated.

This information should make your next social encounter or party more interesting than usual.

Cause and Effect

Say, for example, a person feels negative, defensive, non-participative or hostile. There is a good chance that he will non-verbally signal this with arms crossed on his chest. We also know from research that in a crossed-arms position a person's retention of what he hears is about 40 per cent less and that his attitude becomes more critical.

Now try this simple experiment. Sit back and tightly cross your arms on your chest. How do you feel? Restrained? Non-involved? Non-participative? Studies also show that if you cross your arms because you are cold or for any other reason you begin experiencing the negative effects of this gesture. It is a cause and effect situation. Habitual arm-crossers always say they feel 'comfortable' — any gesture is comfortable when you have a corresponding mental attitude. Even if you don't believe that crossing arms is a negative signal, your listener will unconsciously decode you as negative anyway. And you will never convince a group of people in a cold room.

Learning to Read Body Language

Body language is like a jigsaw puzzle — most of us have many of the pieces but have never put them together to form a picture. Watching television with the sound turned off is an effective way to improve your reading skills. In this way you are forced to observe only the non-verbal medium which sends 60 to 80 per cent of the message. We also recommend *Body Language: How to Read Others' Thoughts by Their Gestures* or *Signals: How to use Body Language for Power, Success and Love* as comprehensive guides to body language.

Finally, always remember the Number One rule of body language—never interpret gestures in isolation, always look for clusters.

Now look at this illustration again. What do you see?

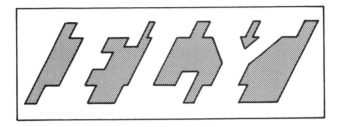

References

Adler, R. *Confidence in Communication*. New York: Holt, Rinehart and Winston, 1977.

Alberti, R. E., and M. L. Emmons. *Your Perfect Right*, 3rd ed. San Luis Obispo, Calif.: Impact, 1978.

Anthony, S. 'Immediacy and non-immediacy: factors in communicating interpersonal attraction.' *Journal of Social Psychology* 93 (1974).

Arkowitz, H. 'Measurement and modification of minimal dating behavior' in M. Hersen, R. Eisley, and P. Miller, eds., *Progress in Behavior Modification*. New York: Academic Press, 1977.

Asch, S. 'Studies of independence and conformity.' *Psychological Monographs* 70 (1956).

Bach, G. R., and R. M. Deutsch, *Pairing: How to Achieve Genuine Intimacy*. New York: Avon, 1971.

Bandura, A. *Social Learning Theory*. Englewood Cliffs, N.J.: Prentice-Hall, 1977.

Bem, D. *Beliefs, Attitudes, and Human Affairs*. Belmont, Calif.: Brooks/Cole, 1970.

Berger, C., and R. J. Calabrese. 'Some explorations in initial interaction and beyond: toward a developmental theory of interpersonal communication.' *Human Communication Research* 1 (1975).

Berne, E., *Games People Play*. New York, Grove Press, 1964.

Berscheid, E., and E. Walster. *Interpersonal Attraction*. Reading, Mass.: Addison-Wesley, 1969.

Birdwhistell, R.L., *Kinesics and Context*. London, Allen Lane, 1971.

Bloom, L. Z., K. Coburn and J. Pearlman. *The New Assertive Woman*. New York: Delacorte, 1975.

Bolton, R. *People Skills: How to Assert Yourself, Listen to Others and Resolve Conflicts*. Englewood Cliffs, N.J.: Prentice-Hall, 1979.

Bower, S., and G.H. Bower. *Asserting Yourself: A Practical Guide to Positive Change*. Reading, Mass.: Addison-Wesley, 1976.

Boyd, L. A., and A. J. Roach. 'Interpersonal communication skills differentiating more satisfying from less satisfying marital relationships.' *Journal of Counseling Psychology* 24 (1977).

Calero, H., *Winning the Negotiation*. New York, Hawthorn Books, 1979.

Carnegie, D., *How to Win Friends and Influence People*. Sydney, Angus and Robertson, 1965.

Chaikin, A. L., and V. J. Dirlega. *Self-Disclosure*. Morristown, N.J.: General Learning Press, 1974.

Clark, J., and H. Arkowitz. 'Social anxiety and self-evaluation of interpersonal performance.' *Psychology Reports* 36 (1975).

Cotler, S., and J. Guerra. *Assertion Training*. Champaign, Ill.: Research Press, 1976.

Cozby, P. C. 'Self-disclosure, reciprocity and liking.' *Sociometry* 35 (1972).

Darwin, C., *The Expression of Emotion in Man and Animals*. New York, Appleton-Century-Crofts 1872.

Duncan, S., and Fiske, D. W., *Face-to-Face Interaction*. Hillsdale, New Jersey, Elrbaum, 1977.

Duck, S. W., and C. Spenser. 'Personal constructs and friendship formation.' *Journal of Personality and Social Psychology* 1972.

Dyer, W. *Your Erroneous Zones*. New York: Funk and Wagnalls, 1976.

Eisler, R., P.Miller, and M. Hersen. 'Components of assertive behavior.' *Journal of Clinical Psychology* 29 1973.

Ellis, A. *Growth Through Reason*. Palo Alto, Calif.: Science and Behavior Books, 1971.

Ellis, A. 'Rational-emotive therapy: research data that supports the clinical and personality hypotheses of RET and other modes of cognitive-behavior therapy.' *The Counseling Psychologist* 7, 1977.

Ellis, A. *Reason and Emotion in Psychotherapy*. New York: Lyle Stuart, 1962.

Ellis, A. and R. Harper, *A New Guide to Rational Living*. North Hollywood, Calif.: Wilshire, 1977.

Fensterheim, H., and J. Baer. *Don't Say Yes When You Want to Say No*. New York: Dell, 1975.

Frankl, Viktor, *Man's Search for Meaning: An Introduction to Logotherapy*. New York: Pocket Books, 1963.

Gambrill, E., and C. Richey. *It's Up to You: Developing Assertive Social Skills*. Millbrae, Calif.: Les Femmes, 1976.

Garner, A. *Conversationally Speaking*, New York, McGraw-Hill, 1980.

Giannandrea, V., and K. Murphy. 'Similarity of self-disclosure and return for a second interview.' *Journal of Counseling Psychology* 20, 1973.

Gibb, J. 'Defensive communication.' *Journal of Communication* 11, 1961.

Glaser, S. R. *Toward Communication Competency*. New York: Holt, Rinehart and Winston, 1980.

Glass, C., J. Gottman and S. Shmurak. 'Response acquisition and cognitive self-statement modification approaches to dating skills training.' *Journal of Counseling Psychology* 23, 1976.

Goffman, E. *Interaction Ritual*. New York: Doubleday-Anchor, 1967.

Goldfried, M., E. Decenteceo and L. Weinberg. 'Systematic rational restructuring as a self-control technique.' *Behaviour Therapy* 5, 1974.

Goldfried, M., and D. Sobocinski. 'Effects of irrational beliefs on emotional arousal.' *Journal of Consulting and Clinical Psychology* 43, 1975.

Goldsmith, J., and R. McFall. 'Develoment and evaluation of an interpersonal skills training program for psychiatric patients.' *Journal of Abnormal Psychology* 84, 1975.

Goldstein, A., and F. Kanfer, eds. *Helping People Change: Methods and Materials*. New York: Pergamon Press, 1975.

Gordon, T. *Parent Effectiveness Training*. New York: Wyden, 1970.

Griffin, K. and S. Gilham. 'Relationships between speech anxiety and motivation.' *Speech Monographs* 38, 1971.

Guerney, B. G., Jr., ed. *Relationship Enhancement*. San Francisco: Jossey-Bass, 1977.

Haley, J., ed. *Strategies of Psychotherapy*. New York: Grune and Stratton, 1963.

Hall, E. *The Silent Language*. New York: Fawcett, 1959.

Hart, R. P., R. E. Carlson, and W. F. Eadie. 'Attitudes toward communication and the assessment of rhetorical sensitivty.' *Communication Monographs* 47 1980.

Hatch, E. J., and B. G. Guerney, Jr. 'A pupil relationship enhancement program.' *Personnel and Guidance Journal* 54, 1975.

Haynes, L. A., and A. W. Avery. 'Training adolescents in self-disclosure and empathy skills.' *Journal of Counseling Psychology* 26, 1979.

Highlen, P. S., and N. L. Voight. 'Effects of social modeling, cognitive structuring, and self-management strategies on affective self-disclosure.' *Journal of Clinical Psychology* 25, 1978.

Homans, G. *Social Behaviour: Its Elementary Forms*. New York: Harcourt, Brace, Jovanovich, 1974.

Hosford, R. E. 'Self-as-a-model: a cognitive social learning technique.' *The Counseling Psychologist* 9, 1980.

Hosman, S., and C. Tardy. 'Self-disclosure and reciprocity in short- and long-term relationships: an experimental study of evaluational and attributional consequences.' *Communication Quarterly* 28, 1980.

Jakubowski, P., and A. Lange. *The Assertive Option*. Champaign, Ill: Research Press, 1978.

Johnson, D. 'Communication and the inducement of cooperative behavior in conflicts: a critical review.' *Speech Monographs* 41, 1974.

Johnson, D., and M. Moonan. 'Effects of acceptance and reciprocation of self-disclosure on the development of trust.' *Journal of Counseling Psychology* 19, 1972.

Johnson, W. *People in Quandaries*. New York: Harper and Row, 1946.

Jourard, S. *The Transparent Self.* New York: Van Nostrand, 1971.

Kazdin, A. 'Effects of covert modeling and model reinforcement on assertive behaviour.' *Journal of Abnormal Psychology* 83 (1974).

Kendon, A., *Organisation of Behaviour in Face-to-Face Interaction,* The Hague, Mouton, 1975.

Knapp, M. *Nonverbal Communication in Human Interaction.* New York: Holt, Rinehart and Winston, 1972.

Kranzler, G. *You Can Change How You Feel.* Eugene, Oreg.: RETC Press, 1977.

Krivonos, P. D. 'The effects of attitude similarity, spatial relationship, and task difficulty on interpersonal attraction.' *The Southern Speech Communication Journal* 45, 1980.

La France, M., and C. Mayo. 'A review of nonverbal behaviors of women and men.' *Western Journal of Speech Communication* 43, 1979.

LaRusso, D. A. *The Shadows of Communication.* Dubuque, Iowa: Kendall/Hunt, 1977.

Lange, A. J., and P. Kaubowski. *Responsible Assertive Behavior: Cognitive/Behavioral Procedures for Trainers.* Champaign, Ill.: Research Press, 1976.

Lazarus, A., ed. *Clinical Behavior Therapy.* New York: Brunner/Mazel, 1972.

Lazarus, A., and A. Fay. *I Can If I Want To.* New York: Morrow, 1975.

Lieberman, R. P., L. W. King, W. J. DeRisi, and M. McCann. *Personal Effectiveness.* Champaign, Ill.: Research Press, 1976.

Litton-Hawes, E. M. 'A foundation for the study of everyday talk.' *Communication Quarterly* 25, 1977.

Mager, R. *Goal Analysis.* Belmont, Calif.: fearon, 1972.

McAllister, H. A. 'Self-disclosure and liking: effects for senders and receivers.' *Journal of Personality* 48, 1980.

McCroskey, J. C. 'Oral communication apprehension: a summary of recent theory and research.' *Human Communication Research* 4, 1977.

McFall, R. and D. Lillesand. 'Behavior rehearsal with modeling and coaching in assertive training.' *Journal of Abnormal Psychology* 77, 1971.

McFall, R. and C. Twentyman. 'Four experiments on the relative contribution of rehearsal, modeling and coaching to assertive training.' *Journal of Abnormal Psychology* 81, 1973.

Mehrabian, A. *Silent Messages.* Belmont, Calif.: Wadsworth, 1971.

Miller, S., D. Wackman, E. Nunally, and C. Saline. *Straight Talk.* New York: Rawson, Wade, 1981.

Morris, D., *Intimate Behavior.* New York: Random House, 1971.

Morris, D., *Manwatching.* London, Cape, 1977.

Morris, D., with Collett, Marsh and O'Shaughnessy, *Gestures, Their Origins and Distribution.* London, Cape, 1979.

Nierenberg, G., and H. Calero, *How to Read a Person Like a Book*, New York, Hawthorn Books, 1971.

Pearce, W., and S. Scharp. 'Self-disclosing communication.' *Journal of Communication* 23 (1973).

Pease, A. V., *The Hot Button Selling System*. Sydney, Camel Publishing, 1976.

Pease, A. V., *Body Language—How to Read Others' Thoughts by Their Gestures*, Sydney, Camel Publishing, 1981.

Phillips, G., and N. Metzger. *Intimate Communication*. Boston: Allyn and Bacon, 1976.

Phillips, G. 'The reticence syndrome: some theoretical considerations about etiology and treatment.' *Speech Monographs* 40, 1973.

Powell, B. *Overcoming Shyness*. New York: McGraw-Hill 1979.

Rehm, L., and A. Marston. 'Reduction of social anxiety through modification of self-reinforcement.' *Journal of Consulting Psychology* 32, 1968.

Rogers, C. R. *On Becoming a Person*. Boston: Houghton-Mifflin, 1961.

Rosenfeld, Lawrence. 'Self-disclosure avoidance: why I am afraid to tell you who I am.' *Communication Monographs* 46, 1979.

Sathre, F., R. Olson and C. Whitney, *Let's Talk*, Glenview, Illinois, Scott Foresman, 1973.

Scherwitz, L., and R. Helmreich. 'Interactive effects of eye contact and verbal content on interpersonal attraction in Dyads.' *Journal of Personality and Social Psychology* 25, 1973.

Sermat, V., and M. Smyth. 'Content analysis of verbal communication in the development of a relationship.' *Journal of Personality and Social Psychology* 26, 1973.

Skinner, B. F. *About Behaviorism*. New York: Knopf, 1971.

Skinner, B. F., *Beyond Freedom and Dignity*. New York: Knopf, 1971.

Skinner, B. F., *Verbal Behavior*. New York: Appleton-Century-Crofts, 1957.

Smith, M. J. *When I Say No, I Feel Guilty*. New York, Dial, 1975.

Strayhorn, J. M., Jr. *Talking It Out*. Champaign, Ill.: Research Press, 1977.

Tubbs, S. L., and S. Moss. *Human Communication*. New York: Random House, 1977.

Twentyman, C., and R. McFall. 'Behavioral training of social skills in shy males.' *Journal of Consulting and Clinical Psychology* 43, 1975.

Wassmer, A. *Making Contact*. New York: Dial, 1978.

Watzlawick, P., J. Beavin, and D. Jackson, *Pragmatics of Human Communication*. New York: Norton, 1967.

Wilmot, W. *Dyadic Communication: A Transactional Perspective*. Reading, Mass.: Addison-Wesley, 1975.

Wolfe, J., and I. Fodor. 'A cognitive behavioural approach to modifying assertive behavior in women.' *The Counseling Psychologist* 5, 1975.

Wolpe, J., and A. Lazarus. *Behavior Therapy Techniques*. London: Peragmon, 1966.

Zimbardo, P. *Shyness: What It Is and What to Do About It*. Reading, Mass.: Addison-Wesley, 1977.

Do you wish your partner came with an instruction manual?

**Why Men Don't Listen &
Women Can't Read Maps**

Explores the differences between men and women in the humorous style of writing we associate with Allan and Barbara Pease. This amazing book has sold more than 12 million copies worldwide!

Revealed in this book:

- Why men can only do one thing at a time
- Why women talk so much
- Why women need love, but men want sex
- Why men won't ask for directions
- How to get the opposite sex to do what you want them to do

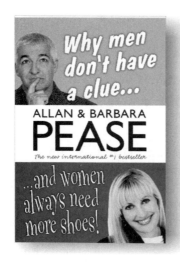

Why Men Don't Have A Clue And Women Always Need More Shoes!

Why are men clueless about romance, love and relationships? Why do they avoid commitment? Why do men tell lies to women and think they can get away with it? On the other hand, why do women cry to get their own way with men and why do women insist on talking a subject to death? And why do women need more shoes instead of sex? The gulf between the sexes, the misunderstandings and conflicts are still as present in our lives in the twenty-first century as they were when Adam first fell foul of Eve. Let Allan and Barbara Pease, the internationally renowned experts in human relations, communication and body language, help you transform the way in which you relate to the opposite sex.

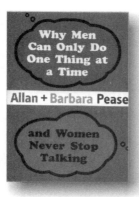

Why Men Can Only Do One Thing At A Time & Women Never Stop Talking

For anyone who has ever laid awake at night wondering why their partner just doesn't understand! The little book of sound advice from the world's foremost experts in relationships....
The perfect hardcover gift book!

www.PeaseInternational.com

HOT DVDs and CDs

Best of Body Language
A 60 minute DVD showing the highlights of over 15 years of hilarious television, based on the No:1 best–selling book. This programme uses hidden cameras, live audience participation and newsreel of various human miscommunications, including real fight scenes, business interviews and people telling real lies!

How to Develop Powerful Communication Skills -
Managing The Differences Between Men & Women
Containing a DVD and two CDs this programme shows:

- What men and women need to do to get on in business
- Why women read minds and men won't ask for directions
- The male boss; his female staff and the cold war
- How to avoid arguments, conflicts and disagreements
- Female Intuition; the walking radar detector
- How to persuade the opposite sex to say 'yes'

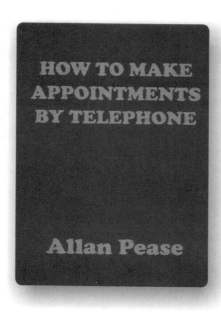

How To Make Appointments By Telephone (CD Pack)

Your phone can create lots of cash. This is an amazingly cost-effective, flexible and dynamic technique that will bring you spectacular results. This technique is used by many of the world's largest sales organisations and promises an average success rate of 7 out of 10 on cold calls. This is the most powerful appointment making tool you'll ever see!

Questions are The Answers

(CD or Cassette) Top level networkers are not 'natural' or 'born'. Top level networking is a skill - a learnable skill, and *QUESTIONS ARE THE ANSWERS*, gives you the techniques and shows you how to use them, how to measure and improve your progress and what to observe when dealing with people. Now available to Direct Selling Groups around the world, this is one of the best training and development products ever. This is THE sales programme to own and comes with a double sided laminated "Priorities Card'.
GET YOURS TODAY!

BUSINESS BOOKS

The Definitive Book of Body Language

This best-selling book isolates, examines and explains in simple terms, each component of body language. Regardless of your vocation or position in life, you will be able to use it to obtain a better understanding of life's most complex event - a face-to-face encounter with another person. It will make you more aware of your own non-verbal cues and signals, and will show you how to use them to communicate effectively and how to get the reactions you want.

Write Language

Both in your business and your personal life, you'll discover that WRITE LANGUAGE is a unique and powerful book. It's a superb investment.

This book shows you amongst other things:

- How to persuade your readers to do what you want them to do
- How to get immediate attention from your reader
- How to make money through direct mail letters.

No matter how many letters you write, this book will help you communicate more effectively.

Talk Language

Some people are so busy 'communicating' that they don't listen to each other.

TALK LANGUAGE tells you how to understand what people are really saying, and why. It shows you how to decode a wide range of everyday signals, so you can get the message or intentions a speaker is really conveying – whether intentionally or not.

TALK LANGUAGE will help you to express yourself clearly and concisely. Its message can be applied to almost every facet of everyday life. You'll learn:

- How to ask powerful questions
- How to make intelligent buying decisions
- How to resist being manipulated
- How to sound interesting and appealing

THIS IS THE SALES BOOK TO OWN.

Questions Are The Answers

The Direct Marketing Business has evolved virtually overnight without fanfare or advertising and could eventually become the largest business system of them all. Its success has been based on the referral-based distribution system and is driven almost entirely by the enthusiasm of its members. It is one of the most dynamic opportunities ever created by the mind of man, and Allan Pease has given everyone the key to unlock this system.

Allan Pease as a Speaker for your next conference or seminar.

With Allan Pease we guarantee that you will **listen, laugh and learn**.

Your attendees will be entertained.

Your attendees will be motivated.

Your attendees will take inspiration home that will last.

Why?

Allan Pease is natural, amiable and dynamic. But don't take it just from us:

"Having such a diverse group of people from the Asia Pacific region can be a little daunting for any speaker. Your presentation was fun, exciting, inspirational, controversial and a topic of conversation between participants for the next few days."
Hewlett-Packard Asia Pacific

"When Allan Pease entertained us at our staff breakfast, his message not only appealed but enriched the personal and professional lives of staff from the Chief Executive to the Managers to the Tradespeople and the Greenkeepers."
Australian Jockey Club

"He is a great communicator and a wonderful entertainer. On more than one occasion, the delegates have told me, they didn't want him to finish."
Wella (UK) Ltd

"Once again our Annual Meeting is behind us and over 6000 members have grown because of the experience."
Million Dollar Round Table USA

www.PeaseInternational.com